Get Carrey-ed away!

From class clown to critical acclaim—Jim Carrey's one actor who has truly captured the attention of television and movie audiences. Early fans remember his first forays into innovative sketch comedy on *In Living Color*, or the runaway success of the sleeper hit *Ace Ventura, Pet Detective*. At first it seemed that Carrey, with his inimitable talent for mimicry and slapstick, was truly born for comedy.

But the ambitious star constantly challenged himself and soon proved to the world that he could tackle serious and thought-provoking subject matter like *The Truman Show*. Of course, one would expect no less from someone precocious enough to have written himself a check for ten million dollars—before he'd even landed his first movie gig!

In *Jim Carrey: Fun and Funnier* you'll find out everything you need to know about this superstar's amazing, rags-to-riches rise to the top—and even about his plans for the future! Quizzes, gossip, anecdotes—it's all in here!

D1431810

Look for other celebrity biographies from Archway Paperbacks and Pocket Pulse

Fun and Funnier:

jim CARREY

NANCY KRULIK

POCKET PULSE
New York   London   Toronto   Sydney   Singapore

An *Original* Publication of POCKET BOOKS

 POCKET PULSE published by
Pocket Books, a division of Simon & Schuster, Inc.
1230 Avenue of the Americas, New York, NY 10020

Copyright © 2000 by Nancy Krulik

ISBN: 0-7434-2218-X

First Pocket Pulse printing December 2000

10 9 8 7 6 5 4 3 2 1

POCKET PULSE and colophon are trademarks of Simon & Schuster, Inc.

Front cover photo by Armando Gallo/Retna

Printed in the U.S.A.

For Ian, the family funny man

Contents

Fun and Funnier:

jim CARREY

A PROMISE KEPT

IT WAS AN EARLY morning in 1985. Jim Carrey had just come off another late night shift at one of the L.A. comedy clubs. Usually Jim just went home after a gig, but on this particular night he swung his old Toyota toward ritzy Mulholland Drive in Hollywood Hills. He parked his car, stared down at the city below, and allowed himself to drift off into a fantasy world in which he was one of the stars rich enough to live in "the Hills."

Jim had come to Los Angeles to make his professional dreams come true. Sure, he liked being a stand-up comic—the sound of a live audience laughing at his impressions and jokes kept him charged up—but he imagined much more. He wanted to be an actor. And he didn't just plan on doing comedy films, either. He wanted to try his hand at more serious fare as well. Someday he hoped TV and movie audiences would learn to love him as much as the people who flocked to the comedy clubs to see him strut his stuff night after night.

Sitting there in the early morning haze, Jim took out his checkbook and wrote a check for ten million dollars, payable to Jim Carrey on Thanksgiving 1995. The note in the memo read, "For acting services rendered." Jim stared at the postdated check for a while before folding it carefully and tucking it in his wallet for safekeeping.

Writing that check was a symbol of Jim's eternal optimism. At that time, Jim barely had ten thousand dollars in his bank account, never mind ten million! But he planned on making it big. He expected to be a star of major proportions, someday earning at least ten million dollars. Of course the irony today is that Jim's actual success has overshot his ten-million-dollar goal many times over. His usual salary now stands at about twenty million dollars per film.

The road to megasuccess has not been smooth for Jim Carrey. Over and over again, he has come up against roadblocks and failures that would have turned an ordinary man away from showbiz and into a life of selling insurance or something equally safe. But of course Jim Carrey is no ordinary man. He's a fighter who has a deep belief in his own talent and a conviction that in the end talent will win out.

"It's always been my pattern," he told *Entertainment Weekly*. "I try something, totally suck, go away, and come back. And then I kill."

That's an understatement. In the past ten years, Jim Carrey has starred in everything from innovative television (*In Living Color*) to record-breaking comedy films (*The Mask, Dumb and Dumber*) to intense dramas that have allowed him to stretch his talent as an actor (*The Truman Show, Man on the Moon*). Along the way he's won two Golden Globe awards and the hearts of millions of fans.

Still, Jim never did get to buy himself that house on Mulholland Drive. Don't feel too bad for him, though—he now lives in a mansion in the ultra-chic Brentwood section of town.

Awards. Mansions. Huge bank accounts. Not bad for a skinny Canadian kid who had to quit school to help his homeless family stay alive. Jim Carrey's life is a true rags-to-riches story. Not even the movies could make up a tale with this much drama. It could only happen in real life—in Jim Carrey's life!

Chapter 1

A Chip Off the Old Block

James Eugene Carrey was born on January 17, 1962 in Newmarket, Ontario, Canada, a small town about 30 miles outside of Toronto. By the time of Jim's arrival, there were already three other small Carreys in the household—Jim's older brother, John, and his two sisters, Pat and Rita.

Jim's dad, Percy, was a saxophone player who'd led a jazz band when he was a teenager. Jim's mom, Kathleen, known as Kay, had been a singer with the band. After they got married, Percy put down his sax and took up the respectable and responsible trade of bookkeeping. Kathleen worked as a hairdresser for a while, but she eventually traded in her scissors for motherhood.

Although Percy left the showbiz life behind when he got married, he still had the makings of an entertainer in his soul. He was a funny man who loved an audience. He was a major joke teller and a practical

5

joker. No one, not even Percy's own family, was exempt from his endless stream of gags. One of his favorites was letting the kids' pet mouse loose from its cage, just to watch Kathleen leap up on a chair in fear.

Percy adored making people laugh, and he loved it when others could crack him up as well. That's part of the reason Percy was so partial to his younger son. Even as a baby, Jim was funny. Sitting in his high chair, he would contort his face into all sorts of shapes when he didn't like the food that was put in front of him. The baby's crazy faces would send Percy into endless bouts of laughter.

As he grew older, Jim continued to make faces. He'd stand in front of the mirror for hours, trying to mimic the facial expressions of his favorite actors.

"It would drive my mother crazy," Jim recalls. "She used to try to scare me by saying that I was going to see the devil if I kept looking in the mirror. That fascinated me even more, of course."

In fact, Jim was so happy making faces in the mirror that the usual childhood punishment of being sent to your room had no meaning for him. "I always had too much fun up there," he laughs. "To punish me you had to send me out to play with other kids."

According to his biography from the press kit for Jim's first TV series, *The Duck Factory*, Jim's first celebrity impersonation was of the late movie star John Wayne. Jim's dead-on impression of the man they called the Duke was especially remarkable considering the fact that Jim was only eight years old at the time. Percy's pride at his young son's talent for mimicry was indescribable.

Surprisingly, though, Jim credits his mom, and not his dad, with his ability to make people laugh. Kay spent much of Jim's childhood in bed, suffering from a series of illnesses. Looking back on it, Jim has told reporters that while some of Kay's illnesses were genuine, others were psychosomatic. "My mother was a professional sick person," he once said. "She took a lot of pain pills. There are many people like that. It's just how they are used to getting attention. I always remember that she's the daughter of alcoholics who would leave her alone at Christmastime."

Jim spent countless hours trying to cheer up his bedridden mother. He put together whole comedy routines in which he did impressions of actors like John Wayne, Don Adams, and Frank Gorshin, who played the Riddler on TV's *Batman*— a sign of things to come! Sometimes, Jim's little shows went on for almost an hour. Often Percy would join in, adding his unique brand of humor to the performance. "My father was really funny and I guess it was a competitive sort of thing," Jim admits.

If Percy was trying to boost his son's confidence, the plan must have worked. When Jim was just ten years old he sent a résumé-like letter to comedienne Carol Burnett, who had a popular comedy-variety show on the air at the time. Carol didn't hire the ambitious ten-year-old. Wonder if she's sorry now.

When Jim was ready to start school, the Carrey family moved to Willowdale, Canada, another suburb of Toronto. Young James Eugene was the new kid in town, and he didn't have many friends. He was shy and so incredibly skinny that the other kids called him Jimmy Gene the String Bean. But Jim soon discovered a wonderful way of winning them over.

"I didn't have any friends until I started hamming it up at the back of the class," he says, remembering his early days at Blessed Trinity Elementary School. "I realized I could do something silly and make people laugh. Then they'd talk to me." One of Jim's early tricks was to chew up a whole handful of colorful candies and then pretend to get sick—spewing a rainbow of candy across the room.

By second grade, Jim had developed quite a reputation as a class clown. Some teachers were frustrated by his wackiness, but Jim managed to find a way to charm them as well. He remembers one class in particular. "I was in music class, and we were practicing for the Christmas assembly. One day I started fooling around, mocking the musicians on the record," he told *Movieline* magazine. "The teacher thought she'd embarrass me by making me get up and do what I was doing in front of the whole class. So I went up and did it. She laughed, and the whole class went nuts. My teacher asked me to do the routine for the Christmas assembly, and I did."

Jim's performance at that Christmas assembly was a huge success. From that moment on, he knew exactly what he wanted to do with the rest of his life: he wanted to be a performer. "That [assembly] was the beginning of the end," he teases.

But Jim's newfound popularity didn't last. While he was still in elementary school, the Carrey family pulled up stakes and moved again, this time to Burlington, a town near Lake Ontario. Once again, Jim was the new kid, this time at the Saint Francis Xavier school. To make things worse, his mother made him take tap-dancing lessons. Tapping his way through dance numbers was not exactly the macho image Jim longed for. "I spent a lot of time trying to hide my shoes from the other boys on the bus. Humiliation started early for me," Jim recalls—only half jokingly—of his toe-tapping days.

Sometime around fourth or fifth grade, Jim discovered that he had a learning disability called dyslexia. Dyslexia made it difficult for Jim to read, but he eventually learned to compensate for the problem with his phenomenal memory. Still, having a learning disability, and being a new kid who also happened to look like a long, skinny string bean, was tough on Jim. Once again he learned to compensate by joking his classmates into liking him.

Before long, the notes started coming home from school. Many of the teachers at Saint Francis Xavier didn't see Jim as funny. They found him disruptive. Kay tried to persuade her son to tone down the funny business. But as usual, Percy supported his son's desire to entertain, no matter where the stage.

One of the teachers at Saint Francis Xavier was Lucille Dervaitis. Jim came into her class in the 1974–1975 school year. The two clicked almost immediately. Mrs. Dervaitis was crazy about Jim's wild and wacky sense of humor, but she refused to put up with his wisecracks during learning time. Instead, she worked out a compromise that helped both Jim and herself.

"She told me that if I didn't fool around during class I could have fifteen minutes at the end of the day to do a comedy routine," Jim recalls. "Instead of bugging everybody, I'd figure out my routine. And at the end of the day, I'd get to perform in front of the entire class. I thought it was really smart of her. It's amazing how important that was."

Performing for the kids in his class was a huge ego boost for Jim. The kids loved his act so much that they would beg for special permission for Jim to perform at other times of the day as well. But Mrs. Dervaitis wasn't falling for it. Jim could perform at the end of the day and that was all.

Jim loved the sound of applause. The more praise he got for his many routines, the more he wanted to perform. In fact, with each end-of-the-schoolday performance, Jim's desire to become a professional comic grew stronger. Unlike most teens, Jim Carrey already knew what he wanted to be when he grew up.

So imagine his surprise when his dad suggested that maybe Jim wouldn't have to wait that long to fulfill his dream.

Chapter 2

YUK YUK, YIKES!

IN 1976, TORONTO GOT its first comedy club: Yuk Yuk's Komedy Kabaret. Yuk Yuk's wasn't really much of a club—just a long skinny room in a community center. But to Percy Carrey, Yuk Yuk's was a dream come true—a place for his youngest son to show off his talent, and a spot for Percy to perform in front of an audience once again. It had been a lot of years since Percy had played with his jazz band, but he'd never lost the desire to get back on the stage. Now he had a chance to fulfill his own dream while helping his son take the first step to success.

It wasn't hard for a comic to get booked at Yuk Yuk's Komedy Kabaret. The club was open once a week. On that one night there was a single professional performer who actually got paid. The rest of the evening was filled with amateur performers. Anyone who showed up got a chance at the microphone.

When Jim was fourteen, Percy convinced him to

try out one of his acts at Yuk Yuk's. It didn't take a lot of persuading. After all, Jim figured that if his classmates thought he was funny, a roomful of strangers would, too. Besides, it was a chance to make his dad proud. Pleasing his parents was something Jim loved more than anything.

Percy was so excited about Jim's debut that he spent hours working with Jim on a new act, while at the same time working on an act of his own. With Percy's support, Jim felt secure enough to walk into the club and get onstage. That's not something your average fourteen-year-old would do. But then again, Jim didn't come from your average family.

"I got a lot of support from my parents," Jim remembers. "That's the one thing I always appreciated. They didn't tell me I was being stupid [when he did his impressions and made wild funny faces]. They told me I was being funny."

When the big night arrived, Percy and Jim went down to Yuk Yuk's together. The father-and-son team sat in the back of the small basement club and waited impatiently for a chance to go onstage and perform some of their material.

Finally somebody passed the mike to Percy. Jim's fun-loving dad got onstage and told a bunch of slightly bawdy jokes to the crowd. He didn't get a whole lot of laughs, but he didn't get booed or heckled, either.

Too bad Jim couldn't claim the same honor. From the moment the skinny, nervous teenager took to the stage, the smell of disaster was in the air. The truth was, the jokes that made teenagers laugh—like the time Jim pulled his shirt over his knees and claimed to be Dolly Parton—didn't have any effect on a crowd of adults. Before long, the audience grew weary of Jim's wild antics and silly impressions. To them he was just some goofy kid.

Stand-up comedy is one of the toughest jobs in show business. Unlike theater, where audiences tend to live by a code that includes silence and attentiveness, comedy club audiences are always ready and willing to be part of the act. They have no problem booing a comic or badgering him with catcalls and worse. Because Jim had only performed for friends and family in the past, he'd never experienced anything but adoration. He was caught off guard when the audience heckled and booed him. Instead of using witty comebacks to counteract the audience's attack, Jim got goofier and goofier. The effect was just plain embarrassing.

The memory of that night was embedded in Jim's brain. Years later he recalled the terror he felt. "The owner of the club had this little thing that he liked to do where he would stand backstage with a microphone and heckle new comedians," Jim told a reporter. "So when I got up there it was just horrendous. He was backstage going 'Totally booooooring!' They were playing excerpts from *Jesus Christ Superstar,* like 'Crucify Him. Crucify Him.' You know, when you go through that kind of experience you kind of develop a thick skin."

That manager, Mark Breslin, would one day actually praise Jim for getting on the stage that night.

"Sure, he bombed, but just think what outrageous confidence it takes for a fourteen-year-old to think he could pull it off in the first place," he told the *London Free Press* years after Jim had gone on to become a successful comic.

Jim, too, would one day be able to put a positive spin on matters. " 'Failure' is a relative term. There isn't failure unless you accept it," Jim told the same *Free Press* reporter. "The ones who make it are the ones who just keep on going."

But that's twenty-twenty hindsight. At the time, Jim wasn't so clear-eyed and objective about his situation. In fact, he was convinced that the night at Yuk Yuk's was the worst of his life. And up until that time, he was probably right. Unfortunately, a lot more bad luck was coming Jim's way.

Chapter 3

WE WERE GYPSIES

LESS THAN A YEAR after his disastrous debut, Jim and his family began a disturbing chapter in their lives that made the night at Yuk Yuk's seem like a walk in the park. In 1977, Percy lost his job, and the Carreys found themselves in the middle of a financial nightmare from which they felt they might never wake up.

At first, the family made do with help from the kids. Pat had already gotten married and moved away, so that was one less mouth to feed. Rita took on baby-sitting assignments to earn grocery money. John also had a part-time job. Jim was still too young to work.

But baby-sitting and part-time work didn't pay much. And it didn't take long for the bills to start piling up. Creditors began knocking at the door of the Carrey house. It was time for the family to pull up stakes and move on.

Percy finally found a job as a night watchman at a factory. As part of the deal, Percy suggested that his family be allowed to work nights at the plant too, in exchange for a place to live. Once the agreement was signed, Jim and his family moved into a farmhouse near the factory.

While Percy guarded the factory, Jim, John, and Rita worked as janitors. It was horrible work, cleaning offices and bathrooms. Jim remembers being very angry. "I hated everyone and everything," he says. "When you're a kid, something like this makes you mad at the world."

It also makes you tired. Unlike other kids in his ninth-grade class, Jim was up working all night. The contract his father had signed included eight-hour shifts for all the members of the Carrey family except Kay, who was frequently too ill to work. Jim had no time for homework or for much sleep. He often got caught dozing off in class. The situation left Jim frustrated.

"I was so angry I didn't want to hear it," he once told *Newsweek* magazine. "I slept in class because I was working in the factory for eight hours after school. I didn't have any friends because I didn't want them. I've gone through periods [as an adult] where I look at street guys and I know that [could have been] me. I know how they got there."

Eventually, Jim quit school. It wasn't doing him any good just sitting there too tired to absorb any information. The fact was, he could have been using the hours he spent in school helping to earn more money for his family.

Had it been any other time in the Carrey family history, Kay and Percy might have objected to Jim's decision to drop out. But at the moment, every dollar helped. Percy and Kay agreed to allow sixteen-year-old Jim to drop out of school.

By the spring of 1978, Percy and Kay decided that their family could no longer work at the factory. Because they lived on the company grounds, the Carreys were treated like indentured servants. They seemed to be on call day and night. The pressure was destroying them. Once again it was time to move on. So Kay and Percy piled the whole family into a yellow Volkswagen van and drove off.

Jim, Rita, and John lived with their parents in the van for almost eight months. For a while, they pitched a tent in Jim's sister Pat's backyard. But mostly they just traveled around.

Surprisingly, Jim doesn't remember life in the van with any bitterness or hostility. It was almost a relief after the drudgery of janitorial work. And there was the joy of being with his parents and two of his siblings. "We had problems like all families," he says. "But we had a lot of love. I was extremely loved. We always felt we had each other."

Of course, that doesn't mean that Jim didn't recognize the absurdity of a whole family traveling around Canada in a Volkswagen van.

"We were Gypsies. It was weird," he admits.

Eventually, the traveling had to come to an end. The Carreys parked their van outside of a small cottage in Jacksons Point, about an hour from Toronto, and went off in search of work. Jim took a job at a picture-framing shop. The other workers at the shop loved Jim. He kept them laughing all day long. The manager of the shop, however, had less affectionate feelings for his new hire. Jim's daily comedy act was keeping people from working. Within six months, Jim was fired.

For most people, being fired is an embarrassing, devastating experience. But in Jim's case it was just the opposite. Being let go from his day job proved one thing: Jim was never going to succeed unless he followed his heart. And his heart wanted to be onstage—and so did the rest of his body, for that matter! He was going to have to get over the trauma he'd experienced at Yuk Yuk's and get back to comedy.

Chapter 4

GETTING YOUR
ACT TOGETHER

NOW, HERE'S ONE FOR the getting-back-on-the-horse department. One of the earliest clubs Jim played when he first returned to stand-up comedy was Yuk Yuk's Komedy Kabaret. By 1978, when Jim was ready to hit the stage again, Yuk Yuk's was a bigger, more famous club. It was no longer located in a community center. It was a full-fledged nightclub in an upscale part of Toronto. And Yuk Yuk's had already launched its first star—Howie Mandel, the comedian who went on to exercise his acting chops on TV's celebrated *St. Elsewhere*.

Naturally, the club had taken on a much more professional air as its reputation grew. Amateur comics were relegated to a late night slot, after the professional headliners had played to the biggest audiences. Beginners had to pay their dues by giving plenty of well-received performances before graduating to paid-performer status.

Looking back, it's kind of amazing that Jim would go back to Yuk Yuk's, of all places, to make his return to nightclub work. To this day, even Jim isn't quite sure how he found the courage to walk back out onto that stage to do a newly refined act consisting of impressions, pratfalls, mugging, and physical comedy rivaled only by circus contortionists. "I have no idea what motivated me to try again," he admits in interviews. "I felt like giving it a shot. Failure taught me that failure isn't the end unless you give up."

Certainly Jim was a different kind of comic at Yuk Yuk's. Most of the performers were into social commentary and political humor. Real highbrow stuff—something that no one has ever accused Jim of. He wasn't the intellectual humor type. He just wanted to make people laugh.

"I'd go on stage with spiked hair and big red pants and just go off," Jim recalls. "Total improvisation."

Many of the jokes Jim told were related to the recent experiences he and his family had lived through. One of his favorites was about a time he asked his dad if the family was poor. The punch line said it all: "No, son. We're rich as long as we have each other. Now get in the Dumpster."

Only a comic genius could turn misery into a great stand-up routine!

To some of the folks who hung out at Yuk Yuk's in 1978, Jim was reminiscent of another young comic who was making it big in the States—Robin Williams. Many people thought Jim had the same sort of wild improvisational spirit that Robin did. And like Robin

Williams, Jim had the kind of physical stamina that is usually reserved for Olympic athletes. He was like the Energizer bunny—he'd keep going and going as long as the audience would listen.

It didn't take long for Jim to progress to the professional level at Yuk Yuk's. The money wasn't great, but it was something, and at least Jim was earning cash doing a job he loved for a change.

Eventually, Jim moved on to other clubs in Canada, like Stitches in Montreal and Giggles, another Toronto club. Jim's dad, Percy, was there for his son every step of the way, acting as his manager and taking a seat in the audience, proudly leading the laughter during each show. Jim's popularity continued to grow, and eventually he found himself headlining at Canadian clubs, sometimes earning upwards of $1,000 a night!

As his following grew, Jim came to the attention of a local agent who booked commercials for radio and TV. In 1981, Jim got his first shot at acting, playing a bad comic on an after-school special called *Introducing Janet*. The hour-long drama explored the relationship between Jim's character, Tony, and Janet (played by Adah Glassbourg), a chubby girl with a pushy mother who has a big problem with low self-esteem.

In the film, Jim actually has to do bad impressions of Groucho Marx and Henry Winkler's Fonzie character from the TV series *Happy Days*. Jim wanted to make sure that people who were not already acquainted with his work realized he was only acting in the film. He assured Canadian *TV Guide* that the

Fonz impression was not his idea. "Wasn't that horrible?" he asked a reporter. "They wrote that. I would never write anything like that. It's ghastly."

As the title of the movie suggests, Jim was hardly the star of *Introducing Janet*. And playing a comedian with little talent and worse timing didn't exactly give him a forum for bringing new audiences into the clubs to see his act. Still, Jim was glad for the opportunity to take his career to a new level and to stretch himself as a performer.

But even with a TV movie to his credit, Jim was still primarily a comic. The clubs were his bread and butter. So in the spring of 1981 Jim leaped at the chance to fly south of the border to New York City to work his maniacal magic on audiences in the Big Apple.

One of the biggest stops Jim made on his whirlwind tour of New York was at Dangerfield's, the comedy club owned by comic legend Rodney Dangerfield. Rodney had won fame in the early 1960s when he appeared on *The Ed Sullivan Show* and managed to make the usually stone-faced Ed Sullivan laugh. He had gone on to become well known for his "I Don't Get No Respect" routine. Rodney's *No Respect* album even won a Grammy for best comedy album in 1980.

As luck would have it, the comic legend just happened to be visiting his club on the night Jim Carrey performed there. Rodney was fascinated by Jim's brand of comedy. He could see that the kid had real talent—even if no one else in the club that night seemed to recognize it.

"Rodney would watch me from the wings, standing there in his housecoat. I'd come offstage and he'd take a drag on his cigarette and shake his head and say, 'They were looking at you like you was from another planet, kid!' " Jim recalled years later.

But Rodney was determined to have Jim's rather unusual kind of comedy seen. He stayed in touch with Jim and arranged for him to be his opening act when Rodney played Canada.

Having Rodney Dangerfield's stamp of approval was a big deal. People respected Rodney and valued his judgment about other comics. Before long, big clubs across America were clamoring for Carrey. In the fall of 1981 Jim took his act on the road to the Mecca of stand-up comedy—Los Angeles.

Chapter 5

CALIFORNIA, HERE HE COMES

IN THE EARLY 1980s, Los Angeles was the place all young comedians dreamed of playing. Not only did the club gigs pay well, but it seemed that every night, hot spots like the Improv and the Comedy Store were packed with network executives looking for comics to appear on variety shows or to take on a comedic role in a TV pilot that was already in development. Getting his own TV show was every comic's dream.

Jim was no exception. He loved playing clubs, but his goals were higher. On his first trip to Los Angeles Jim stopped to look at the handprints and footprints in front of Mann's Chinese Theatre. As Jim studied the names of the stars printed in the cement, he vowed that someday he too would be famous enough to have his handprints on that sidewalk of fame. His prediction did come true, but it took almost fifteen years: Jim added his handprints to the walk outside Mann's Chinese Theatre in 1995.

Jim's first trip to L.A. was highlighted by a successful stint at the Improv. Although he didn't receive any firm offers, Jim did come to the attention of several casting agents, including some people from *The Tonight Show*. The producers of that late night show liked Jim's work a lot, but felt that he needed a little more polish—and fewer dirty jokes—before he would be ready to perform on the same stage with Johnny Carson, who was *The Tonight Show*'s host before Jay Leno took over.

Jim left L.A. at the end of 1981 to do a televised New Year's Eve show for Canadian TV. But the City of Angels had already begun to feel like home. Eventually Jim found himself spending so much time in L.A. that he had to take a room in a house in West Hollywood. His housemates were other aspiring performers who, like Jim, spent a great deal of time on the road.

Jim spent his L.A. nights playing the clubs and honing his act. During the day he took acting classes and auditioned for commercials, movies, and TV shows.

Jim's hard work eventually paid off in the spring of 1982. He was offered a role in the TV movie *Copper Mountain*. He played Bob, a shy guy who starts to do impressions whenever he gets nervous talking to girls.

There wasn't much of a script to *Copper Mountain*, and nobody on the set of the TV movie had any delusions that they were doing *Hamlet*. Still, the movie shoot did offer Jim a chance to learn to ski and to spend some time at a Club Med resort. He also got to meet famed rockers Rita Coolidge and Ronnie Hawkins, both of whom provided songs for the film's sound track.

Jim tried his best to learn what he could from experienced actors like Alan Thicke, who played a fellow guest at the Copper Mountain resort. But Jim had to admit that the thirteen-hour days often got to him. He also had a hard time getting used to the long waits between scenes. "I get so anxious when I have to wait," he explained to a reporter at the time. "Onstage is really where I get my kicks. Being live onstage is the best feeling in the world."

Of course, as everyone now knows, Jim did eventually learn to become more patient and comfortable on movie sets. But his love of live performing has never left him. Today he expresses it by mugging for the paparazzi's cameras or goofing around with the crews on his movies.

By the end of 1982 Jim had decided that if his career was going to go anywhere he had to live in Los Angeles full-time. In January 1983 he moved permanently to L.A. and became a full-fledged member of the comic community. As such there was one place he really wanted to play—the Comedy Store.

The Comedy Store was run by Mitzi Shore, a powerful woman in the stand-up business. She'd built the Comedy Store into a major power in Hollywood. Many of the comics who went on to careers in TV and film were veterans of her stage. So having Mitzi in their corner was extremely important to young comics.

Luckily, Mitzi liked Jim. He was one of her favorites. She found him fresh and exciting, not to mention always respectful of her position as owner of the Comedy Store. Whenever there was a talent scout in the audience, Mitzi made sure Jim was on the bill.

Mitzi Shore wasn't Jim's only influence during his early Los Angeles days. He also found a great teacher and cohort in a loud, edgy comic named Sam Kinison. Sam and Jim were truly comedy's odd couple. Jim was long and lean, and had an act that was based on impressions and physical humor. Sam was small and chunky. His act was filled with loud, shocking screams, and raunchy jokes. But the two men hit it off and remained close friends until Sam's untimely death in a car accident in 1992.

Under Sam's influence, Jim slowly began to move away from doing impressions. He told a reporter for the *Free Press,* "There's going to come a time when just doing impressions won't be enough. I want to do everything."

In 1983 singer Linda Ronstadt came to the Comedy Store to catch Jim's act. One of her backup singers had recommended that Linda check him out. Linda liked what she saw and asked Jim to be the opening act during her upcoming tour. It was an amazing opportunity. Before he knew it, Jim was on the road with Linda.

Despite their age difference—Jim was twenty-one and Linda was thirty-seven—the attraction between the cute comic and the rock diva was powerful. They began a romance during Linda's 1983 tour. The relationship continued after the touring ended, and Jim began spending more and more time living in luxury at Linda's mansion in Brentwood. Waking up in a mansion was a far cry from that Volkswagen van Jim and his family had shared during his teenage years in Canada. Jim knew he could get used to living a life of wealth and privilege.

But getting there wasn't going to be easy. Jim knew that Linda's money came from years and years of hard work. She'd been a major star throughout the 1970s, and her career was still going strong in the 1980s. She toured endlessly and continued to record albums. If Jim wanted to live the way Linda did, he would have to work equally long and hard. But that didn't scare Jim. He certainly wasn't afraid of hard work—nothing would ever seem hard after being a janitor in a factory. Besides, performing was fun; it was more like play than work.

In September 1983, Jim left Linda's side and headed up to Calgary, in Alberta, Canada, to shoot a movie called *Finders Keepers*. Jim was excited about the film because it was based on a fine novel by Charles Dennis called *The Next to Last Train Ride*. Even more exciting was the prospect of working with famed British filmmaker Richard Lester, who'd directed the Beatles in both *A Hard Day's Night* and *Help!* Jim only had a small role in the wacky train chase extravaganza, but he used his time on the set well, learning as much as he could about filmmaking by watching Richard Lester at work.

Jim had high hopes that *Finders Keepers* would catapult him to a new level in Hollywood. But when the movie tanked at the box office, it became clear that this wasn't going to be Jim's ticket to success.

Jim didn't have much time to be depressed about the poor box office reaction to the film, however. A new opportunity soon appeared: Jim was offered the leading role in a situation comedy that was guaranteed to air in prime time on NBC television. Soon Jim would be entering the homes of Americans on a weekly basis. It was the opportunity of a lifetime!

Chapter 6

DUCK!

JIM'S NEW TELEVISION SERIES, *The Duck Factory*, seemed like a guaranteed hit. This sitcom about a young cartoonist was created by Allan Burns who, along with James L. Brooks, had come up with the idea for *The Mary Tyler Moore Show*, a 1970s mega-success. Allan had also been one of the creators of the groundbreaking *Smothers Brothers Comedy Hour* in the 1960s. When it came to quality comedy television, Allan Brooks was the man!

Jim was offered $5,000 an episode to play Skip Tarkenton, a cartoonist from the Midwest who moves to Los Angeles to take on his first job at an animation factory, working on "The Dippy Duck Show." The premise was great, but Jim was miscast. Skip was the straight man of the show, surrounded by wacky characters in much the same way that Mary Tyler Moore was the voice of sanity among her crazy cohorts on

The Mary Tyler Moore Show. Jim just wasn't given a chance to really show off his comedic ability.

Years later Allan Burns would admit that he had wasted Jim's considerable talent. "Had I understood Jim's incredible qualities earlier, I would have reshaped the character rather than forcing him to fit something that had been conceived before he came along," he told one reporter. "It was unfortunate, but by the time we cast him there wasn't time to re-create the character."

Jim shared his newly found good fortune with his parents, asking Percy and Kay to live in the extra bedroom of the small bungalow he'd purchased in North Hollywood. Jim's mom and dad lived there for several months, basking in their son's burgeoning celebrity. Eventually, though, they returned to their native Canada, which would always be home to them.

Part of the premise of the show was that the make-believe "Dippy Duck Show" was always in danger of being canceled. Ironically, almost from its inception *The Duck Factory* found itself in the same mess. From the moment it entered the NBC lineup as a midseason replacement in April of 1984 there were problems. The show was sandwiched in a Thursday night spot between *Cheers* (a comedy that took place in a bar) and *Hill Street Blues* (a one-hour police drama). Both shows were huge hits for the network, but they were already in late season reruns when *The Duck Factory* premiered. That made getting huge ratings almost an impossibility. After just thirteen episodes, NBC pulled the plug on *The Duck Factory*.

Jim was disappointed when he heard that the show was canceled, but he wasn't totally surprised, or brokenhearted, by the network's decision. "I suppose I'd be upset if I was forty and my series was dying," the twenty-two-year-old Jim told Noel Gallagher of the *London Free Press*. "But it's too early in my career to worry. Besides, I believe that things—good or bad—are meant to happen."

There were more bad things in store for Jim. On top of the failure of *Finders Keepers* and the demise of *The Duck Factory,* Jim's love life was a mess. Jim and Linda had broken up in December 1983, while he was working on *The Duck Factory*. That was a mutual decision: Linda eventually went on to date *Star Wars* creator George Lucas, and Jim told friends he was happy to no longer be known in certain circles merely as Linda Ronstadt's boyfriend.

By the summer of 1984 Jim found himself without a steady paycheck or a steady girlfriend. It was obvious that change was in the air. The only question was, which way would the wind blow?

Chapter 7:

MOVIES, MAYHEM, AND MARRIAGE

AFTER THE CANCELLATION OF *The Duck Factory*, Jim took to the road, performing in New Orleans and Las Vegas with veteran mimic Rich Little. This was an honor for Jim. Rich Little was the king of impersonators at that time, and his desire to perform with Jim was an invitation into an elite club.

But Jim had already decided that that was one club he didn't want to join. Jim just couldn't see himself imitating movie stars on the Vegas stage for the rest of his life. It suddenly occurred to Jim that he didn't want to *impersonate* celebrities; he wanted to *be* a celebrity. And to fulfill that dream he was going to have to develop a different kind of comedic style, something daring and exciting that would set him apart from every other comic who had come before him. He wanted to try things that had more bite.

If bite was what Jim wanted, he certainly got his wish in mid-1984, when he was offered a costarring role opposite model Lauren Hutton in the vampire comedy *Once Bitten*.

The movie was a switch on typical vampire flicks in that the vampire was a woman. Lauren's character was known simply as the Countess. Jim played a high school student named Mark who was her source of virgin blood. The Countess had to bite Mark's thigh three times in order to keep her youth and immortality. With each bite, Jim's character became more and more vampirelike. The bizarre changes in Mark's behavior—like a sudden need to scarf down huge amounts of blood-red raw meat—gave Jim a chance to show off his comedic talent in a few scenes. Although Jim was once again stuck in a constraining good-guy role, a few comedic sparks predicted the wacky physical humor that was to surface in Jim's later flicks.

Jim followed up his performance in *Once Bitten* with a small role in a romantic comedy called *Peggy Sue Got Married*. The film starred Kathleen Turner and Nicolas Cage as a married couple who'd been together since high school. In the film, forty-three-year-old Peggy Sue (Kathleen Turner) travels back in time to her senior year in high school to decide whether to marry Charlie (Nicolas Cage), her childhood sweetheart. Jim played Walter Getz, Charlie's best friend. Like almost all of the characters in the film, Jim got to play Walter both in high school during the late 1950s and as an adult in the 1980s, but his screen time was so short that he was barely noticed at all.

Unfortunately, fans will never see Jim's best work during *Peggy Sue Got Married*. That took place behind the cameras, when Jim entertained the cast and crew with bits from his stand-up routine. He was a popular member of the cast despite the fact that his name was rarely on the call sheet. His behind-the-scenes antics may not have made Jim a star, but they did earn him a new friend in Nicolas Cage. To this day the two men are close pals.

After working on *Peggy Sue Got Married*, Jim had no more film projects lined up. So he returned to Mitzi Shore's fold, once again taking the stage at the Comedy Store. Upon his return, Jim discovered that Mitzi had hired a new waitress, an aspiring actress named Melissa Womer, whose blond good looks attracted Jim almost immediately.

Melissa was a big change from Jim's previous girl-friend, Linda Ronstadt, but that was fine with Jim. His whole life was in flux at the time. He was busy redefining himself as a comedian, slowly dropping the impressions from his act and slipping in more bizarre bits like hiding himself inside a piano, just to see how the crowd would react. And while the crowd didn't always seem to get Jim's offbeat humor, Melissa did. That drew the two of them closer together.

On March 28, 1987, Jim and Melissa made their special bond official during an outdoor wedding ceremony in Santa Monica, California. As the sun set on his wedding day, Jim felt incredibly positive. He had a feeling that marrying Melissa was just the beginning of a wonderful new period in his life.

Chapter 8

OH, BABY!

AND BABY MAKES THREE! In September 1988, Jim and Melissa welcomed a baby girl named Jane to their tight-knit family. Jim had goofed around about a lot of things, but he took fatherhood extremely seriously. He'd grown up in an incredibly supportive household, despite the financial turmoil that had often surrounded the family. Jim was determined to give Jane the same love he'd received as a child. He was a totally hands-on dad, diapers and all. It didn't take much to make Jim happy in those days; just being able to make his child laugh brought a smile to Jim's face. And since Jim had never had any trouble making folks laugh, there was a lot of joy in the Carrey household.

Some people say that babies bring luck, and in Jim's case Jane definitely was a rabbit's foot, a four-leaf clover, and a heads-up penny all rolled into one. Not long after her birth, Jim took on a small role in

The Dead Pool, the fifth film in Clint Eastwood's spectacularly popular Dirty Harry series.

The part of Johnny Shakes was tailor-made for Jim's wacky, and sometimes wicked, sense of humor. Johnny Shakes is a leather-clad, spike-haired, drug-addicted, egomaniacal rock singer, who is in the midst of making a hard core rock-and-roll video. Both Clint and the film's director, Buddy Van Horn, agreed to let Jim take the character in any direction he wanted. It was a dangerous deal, considering Jim's sometimes over-the-top humor. But even back then Jim had a strong sense of what would and wouldn't work on film. He managed to make Johnny Shakes a caricature of hard rock singers without turning the character into a cartoon.

Johnny Shakes dies early in *The Dead Pool*, but Jim managed to make his mark, both on and off the screen. Clint Eastwood was so impressed by Jim's performance that he hired him again to play a cameo role in his next film, *Pink Cadillac*. Although neither role was a star-making turn, Jim had found himself a good friend in Clint Eastwood. And let's face it, in Hollywood, Clint's the kind of friend you want to have around. Years later, in 1996, Jim would repay the favor by emceeing the televised ceremony in which Clint received a Lifetime Achievement Award from the American Film Institute.

Jim's excitement at becoming part of Clint Eastwood's distinguished circle of friends was tempered by the sad knowledge that Kay Carrey hadn't lived long enough to share his thrill ride to success.

Jim's mom died in October 1989 at the age of sixty-one.

Losing his mom at a such a young age was painful, but like any good comic, Jim put on a happy face and moved on toward the next project. He was on a roll, and he knew it. So when he read the completely whacked-out script for a sci-fi musical comedy called *Earth Girls Are Easy,* he jumped at the chance to be part of the team. Jim was crazy about the idea of playing a space alien. The part of Wiploc, Alien #2, was perfect for him. After all, Rodney Dangerfield had said all along that audiences looked at Jim as if he was from another planet.

There was another benefit to taking on the part of Alien #2 in *Earth Girls Are Easy:* he got to work with Aliens #1 and #3. Jeff Goldblum was the first alien, and Damon Wayans was cast as #3. Damon and Jim became close friends. Both men saw themselves as comic renegades, always interested in pushing the envelope just a little further.

While Jim, Jeff, and Damon were busy conquering the earth—and movie multiplexes—Damon's brother Keenen was busy creating a series for the newly formed Fox network. It was a sketch comedy show that would take TV audiences in a direction they'd never gone before. Keenen Ivory Wayans wanted the show to be hot, hip, and more than a little off the wall. He envisioned it as a kind of renegade series with a primarily African-American cast.

But when Damon Wayans suggested that Jim meet with Keenen to talk about the show, Jim wasn't very excited at the prospect. Since his quick quack with *The Duck Factory,* he was less than confident about being part of a TV show.

But after auditioning for Keenen and other producers of what would eventually be called *In Living Color,* Jim changed his mind. He could tell that the Wayans brothers had the same silly—some might say sick—take on the world as he did.

And so, when *In Living Color* hit the airwaves on April 15, 1990, Jim Carrey was there, adding to the merriment and mayhem.

Chapter 9

MAKING IT BIG ON THE SMALL SCREEN

JIM WAS RIGHT IN his element with the folks who took part in the weekly laugh fest that was *In Living Color*. The show's ensemble cast included several Wayans family members—Keenen, Damon, and their sister Kim—as well as Tommy Davidson, David Alan Grier, and T'Keyah Keymah. All of the cast members had their own talent for creating wildly fascinating characters and for doing dead-on impressions of famous stars.

In Living Color was the perfect format for Jim's sense of humor. Once again he was able to do impressions. Only this time he could imitate more recent performers and put even more bite into his routines, doing things like turning Vanilla Ice into a psychotic spike-haired weirdo.

Jim was also given carte blanche to come up with original characters all his own. Perhaps his most famous character from the *In Living Color* days was

Fire Marshal Bill, a burned and disfigured pyromaniac who became more and more grossly injured each time he told the audience, "Let me show you something." Despite the character's popularity, Fire Marshal Bill was eventually banished by Fox because the network executives were afraid he was encouraging kids to play with fire.

Jim loved coming up with new characters. Often they came from chance encounters with people Jim met on the street, in the store, or at the gym. "Sometimes a character begins with a spark of somebody's personality," he told reporters at the time. "Then I just pull it, stretch it, and take it as far as I can . . . it's about getting the laughs."

In Living Color was an instant success. Critics raved about its lowbrow, high talent humor combination. *Newsweek* magazine commented that "So far the ratings indicate yet another triumph for TV's most audacious network. Among the with-it young, this weekly satirical revue is fast becoming Saturday night's hottest party ticket."

In 1989–1990 *In Living Color* received an Emmy Award for Outstanding Variety, Music, or Comedy Series and an award from the NAACP. The following year it received the People's Choice Award for Favorite New Television Comedy Series and the Nickelodeon Kids Choice Award for Favorite TV Show (tied with *The Simpsons*). By 1992 *In Living Color*'s popularity had soared so high that Fox had the cast perform live along with

Color Me Badd during the halftime show at the Super Bowl.

Jim was thrilled with the accolades and fame that came with being one of the *In Living Color* regulars. It was like getting paid to play. And his newfound popularity made him a hot commodity. Showtime television approached him about doing a special for their cable network. In the middle of the second season, Jim polished up his stage act and headed back up to Canada, where he performed at the Theatre Passe Muraille in Toronto. The whole show was taped for broadcast on Showtime.

Jim's stand-up routine was filled with more overtly sexual references than anything he did on *In Living Color*. That's the lure of cable: far fewer restrictions are imposed by nervous network censors. He also joked about his parents and his upbringing, and did several of his choicest celebrity impersonations. The special, entitled *Jim Carrey's Unnatural Act*, was broadcast throughout November of 1991. But the reviews and rating were a disappointment to both Jim and Showtime, and the network quickly pulled the special from its schedule.

Jim didn't let the disappointment bring him down. He simply poured himself back into his work at *In Living Color* and let the cheers from the show's fans buoy up his spirits once again. But deep down Jim knew that *In Living Color* couldn't last forever. And if he wanted to have a long-lasting career he'd have to do something more than imitate psychotic pyromaniacs and presidential hopefuls like Ross Perot. "To me, it's the saddest thing in the world to see a comedian at sixty doing the same characters and the same act," Jim told *Time* magazine.

To keep from becoming one of those sad old comedians, Jim decided to exercise his acting chops during the 1992 hiatus from *In Loving Color*. He took on a role in a serious TV movie called *Doing Time on Maple Drive*. Jim played Tim, a twenty-something alcoholic who is tired of living under the demanding rules of his ex–military man dad. Jim was hand-picked for the role by the movie's director, Ken Olin, best known for portraying Michael Steadman on the melodrama series *thirtysomething*. At the time, Ken admitted to reporters that he wasn't familiar with Jim's work on *In Living Color* and was simply blown away by his honest, understated reading at his audition.

Jim's character in *Doing Time on Maple Drive* was carrying around a lot of emotional baggage. He was constantly being criticized by his dad, who would make stinging remarks like "Every time I look at you I thank God I have another son."

The father-son relationship in the movie bore little resemblance to Jim's relationship with the lavishly supportive Percy Carrey, but Jim was still able to draw up enough pain and emotion to make Tim's reactions to his dad's verbal slaps seem real. His portrayal of Tim proved that Jim was more than just a comedian with a gift for mimicry and wacky physical shtick. He was an actor with a true artist's soul.

To this day, many critics think that Jim did some of his best work in *Doing Time on Maple Drive*. A reviewer for WLWT Cincinnati said of Jim's work that "there's no gags and no props, just fine acting."

After the seriousness of the *Maple Drive* set, Jim returned to *In Living Color* ready to go wild. Stretching himself was fine and challenging. But for the time being, the controlled anarchy of *In Living Color* felt like home.

Chapter 10

JIM'S
PET PROJECT

IN 1994, JIM WAS still happily skewering celebrities and society on *In Living Color* when the folks at Morgan Creek productions came to him with an idea for a movie about a detective who specializes in cases involving animals. Jim hadn't been seen on the big screen in almost five years, since *Earth Girls Are Easy*, and yet he was reluctant to do the movie. The problem was simple: he liked the film's premise, but hated the script.

Finally, Jim and the producers came to an understanding: Jim could make changes in the script if he agreed to star in the film. That was the guarantee that Jim needed. He signed on and began rewriting the movie almost immediately, keeping nothing but the initial premise: Detective Ace Ventura goes in search of a missing Miami Dolphins mascot. Other than that, all the new jokes and gags were pure Jim Carrey. Jim was paid $350,000 to write and act in the film.

In the spring of 1993, Jim flew down to Miami to begin filming *Ace Ventura, Pet Detective*. He had a blast, keeping the cast and crew laughing with his off-screen antics. As funny as the movie turned out to be, people who were there during the filming agree that Jim's best bits took place off camera.

Jim's silly, grinning behavior masked a real problem in his life, however. By the time *Ace Ventura* wrapped, Jim and Melissa had officially separated.

Jim took responsibility for the split. He admitted that success had indeed gone to his head and that he'd been tough to live with. "Living with me these last couple of years has been like living with an astronaut," Jim confessed to a magazine. "It's like 'I just came back from the moon. Don't ask me to take out the garbage.' "

Jim's separation from Melissa was anything but simple. There was a lot of wrangling over money. But the one thing neither parent argued about was how to deal with Jane. Jim and Melissa agreed to share custody of their young daughter.

Ace Ventura, Pet Detective was scheduled to be released in February 1994. Jim was extremely anxious about how the movie would be received. He knew it was different from anything that anyone else was doing. But was that a good thing or a bad thing? Only time would tell.

"This is the kind of thing where either they love me or hate me," Jim told a magazine during a whirlwind promotional tour leading up to the release of the film. In the end, the fans loved him and the critics hated

him, and that was okay with Jim. By the second weekend, the film had grossed more than $25 million. He
didn't need to be a critic's darling; just seeing the box
office receipts building higher and higher let him
know that he had his finger on the average moviegoer's pulse. His audience liked things a little raunchy
and lowbrow. Slapstick humor was the way to go. As
for the critics, Jim told *Newsweek* that their opinions
didn't mean much. "I just think, Would I want to go
see a movie with those guys in it?"

Chapter 11 **∴**

PUTTING ON THE MASK

JIM'S FOLLOW-UP TO *Ace Ventura* was an ambitious endeavor—bringing a comic book character to life. The leading role in *The Mask* was perfect for Jim— after all, many people considered him a human cartoon anyway.

Jim was paid $450,000 to play a Jekyll-Hyde character in *The Mask*. For part of the film he was mild-mannered Stanley Ipkiss, a kind of human doormat who lets everyone step on him and take advantage of his weaknesses. But the moment Stanley finds an old Viking mask, the movie changes. He becomes The Mask—a green-faced wild man who sings and dances his way through life in a yellow zoot suit and a huge fedora.

The many special effects in *The Mask* were provided by the famed Industrial Light and Magic company. The ILM technicians searched their bag of special effects tricks and found ways to make Jim's

48

eyeballs pop out of their sockets, and his heart leap out of his chest. At first, Jim worried that the effects would overshadow his performance. But he needn't have been concerned. When *The Mask* (co-starring Cameron Diaz) was released, everyone knew who the real star of the film was. No matter what effects the ILM people created, critics and fans agreed that the film's best special effect was Jim. As Richard Corliss reported for *Time* magazine, "Carrey doesn't need any cybernetics or silicon to rubberize his limbs. He's his own special effect, the first star who is a live-action toon."

When *The Mask* shot to the number one spot in the summer of 1994, Jim was batting two for two. He was now a full-fledged star, and his earnings reflected his status. Jim received $7 million to star in his next comedy, *Dumb & Dumber*. To take on the supporting role of the Riddler in *Batman Forever*, he was paid $5 million—plus a percentage of the profits from toys based on his character.

Getting the part of the Riddler was a big deal for Jim even without the bucks. At the time, everyone thought the part would go to Robin Williams. In fact, Robin was in the middle of negotiations with the producers when they switched gears and offered the role to Jim. All of Hollywood was shocked. But no one was more surprised than Jim, who was in France, promoting *The Mask* at the Cannes Film Festival when he received the call that he'd gotten the part. "When I got the call in Cannes that they wanted me I just couldn't believe it," Jim recalls.

But before he could go to Gotham City to become the Riddler, Jim had to travel to Colorado to begin shooting *Dumb & Dumber*.

Jim had a great on-screen partner in *Dumb & Dumber*. Jim played Lloyd, a really dumb limo driver, while Jeff Daniels played his buddy, Harry, who's even dumber than Lloyd. (Dumb and Dumber, get it?) Jim's on-screen chemistry with Jeff Daniels was indisputable. But it was Jim's *offscreen* chemistry with actress Lauren Holly that made headlines.

Lauren Holly, a beautiful blonde who'd starred on *Picket Fences* and the soap opera *All My Children,* had been cast as a mysterious woman who rides in Lloyd's limo and leaves behind a package. When Lloyd and Harry decide to deliver the package to her, the fun really begins.

Everyone on the set of *Dumb & Dumber* could see that Jim and Lauren were attracted to each other. "They were made for each other," writer-director Peter Farrelly told *People* magazine in the fall of 1994. Charles Rocket, who played Nicholas André in the film, agreed, telling the magazine that "They're like a couple of kids at the beginning of a relationship. Goofing around, laughing at each other's jokes."

Jim was definitely in love again. And this time he was able to enjoy a blossoming relationship without wondering where the next rent check would come from. "The money and stuff is a wonderful thing," Jim told *People*. "I spend it."

Boy, did he ever! In 1994 alone, Jim bought himself a vintage 1965 Thunderbird, and a million-dollar home in Brentwood. But, ever the doting dad, Jim did remember to put cash aside for Jane's college education.

Jim really didn't have to worry about paying Jane's tuition (or buying anything else she might want or need), especially after he signed his next contract—a whopping $20 million deal to do the sequel to *Ace Ventura*. To quote the Mask, Jim's love life and his career were smokin'!

Chapter 12

KA-CHING!

WITH THE MASSIVE SUCCESS of *Dumb & Dumber*
Jim was the indisputable king of gross-out comedies.
But the success of Jim's films was not based solely on
slapstick humor and dirty jokes. There has always
been a heart to Jim's characters, like the scene in
Dumb & Dumber when Lloyd shouts out that he's
"sick and tired of having to eke my way through life.
I'm sick and tired of being nobody. I'm sick and tired
of having nobody!" Director Peter Farrelly told *Time*
magazine that while he was shooting that scene tears
welled up in Jim's eyes during every take. "His emo-
tions are at his fingertips," Peter explained.

Jim's follow-up to *Dumb & Dumber, Batman
Forever,* was released in 1995. Reviews for the film as
a whole were not great, but Jim's over-the-top performance as the Riddler was universally praised.
Despite the mixed reviews, *Batman Forever* was a
huge moneymaker, both in the United States and inter-

nationally. Many movie industry types seemed to feel that it was Jim who brought in the fans.

Ace Ventura, The Mask, Dumb & Dumber, Batman Forever—it seemed Jim had the Midas touch. Every movie he signed on for turned to gold. He had legions of loyal fans. According to Michael Levine, author of a book that lists the addresses of stars, Jim was now receiving more fan mail than any other motion picture star—nearly 50,000 letters a month. *People* magazine named him one of the most intriguing people of 1994, and Barbara Walters interviewed him for her Oscar special in early 1995. It was wild!

Jim could come up with only one explanation for what was happening in his life at that time. "I guess society is a lot more twisted than I thought," he joked.

Jim treated his newfound success with typical sarcastic humor: "I'm thinking of changing my name . . . to Ka-ching—the sound of a cash register."

But Jim's joy at his newfound fame was tempered by the fact that his dad wasn't around anymore to share the excitement. Percy Carrey died in the fall of 1994. Even before his death Percy had been suffering from Alzheimer's disease and probably was never aware of his son's worldwide success. Jim knew that no one would enjoy what was happening in his life the way Percy would have. But Jim had a special way of letting his dad know that he was a success now. Before Percy was buried, Jim placed something special in his father's suit pocket—the $10 million check Jim had made out to himself so long ago, on the night he drove over to Mulholland Drive and dreamed of being a star.

Despite his grief, Jim pushed himself to work on a new project right away. Jim knew he had to follow up his success with a surefire box office success to cement his position in Hollywood. The picture he chose to do, *Ace Ventura: When Nature Calls,* a sequel to *Ace Ventura, Pet Detective,* was a safe bet.

Ace Ventura: When Nature Calls supposedly took place in Africa, but was actually shot on a wild animal preserve in Texas. The location was hot, and the stunts were tough. And of course there was the issue of working with real animals.

"I actually touched one [of the bats]," Jim recalled to *Entertainment Weekly.* "I touched it with my finger. And that's not a smart thing to do. I don't suggest anybody do that. But you know, I'm a professional. That's why I was cast as Ace Ventura."

But all joking aside, Jim was going through tough times. He and Melissa were still in the process of finalizing the divorce. And Jim really missed his parents. It was hard getting used to not looking to them for support and approval.

But Jim never brought his personal problems to the set. In public he seemed to be his old wacky self. Luckily, Lauren Holly spent a lot of time with Jim on the set, giving him a shoulder to lean on when it all seemed too much.

Once *Ace Ventura: When Nature Calls* was finished and ready for release, Jim was all smiles and jokes once again. He was extremely proud of the final effort. "It's sick. It's my ticket to the gates of hell," he bragged. "It's like ten times worse than the first one."

B. Boudreau/Shooting Star

 Jim Carrey reaches for the stars!

Jim then . . .

. . . and now

Ace Ventura

Batman Forever

The Mask

The
Cable Guy

Medieval Times

Medieval Times

Dumb
and Dumber

The
Truman
Show

Me, Myself
& Irene

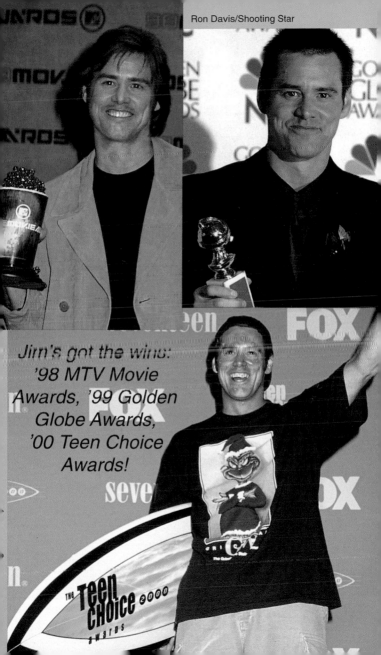

Ron Davis/Shooting Star

Jim's got the wins:
'98 MTV Movie
Awards, '99 Golden
Globe Awards,
'00 Teen Choice
Awards!

Just joking!

Yoram Kahana/Shooting St[a]

B. Boudreau/Shooting Star

Jim knew that *Ace Ventura: When Nature Calls* wasn't going to be the epic *Gone With the Wind* of its generation. He didn't want it to be. All Jim desired was for his audience to have a great time with the movie. "I just want it to be killer funny," he told reporters at the time. "You know, kick ass, piss in your pants, run out of the theater . . . and throw yourself in traffic funny!"

Which is exactly what the film turned out to be. Just as Jim had hoped, the fans loved it so much that *Ace Ventura: When Nature Calls* outgrossed the original *Ace Ventura*—in cash, not just in jokes!

It was obvious that Jim had found his niche in outrageous comedy flicks. So it was confusing to many Hollywood types when Jim announced that his next project would be Ben Stiller's dark, angry film, *The Cable Guy*. Even though Jim was being offered $20 million to make the film, plenty of insiders thought it was a mistake for Jim to play against type. That's a big no-no in Hollywood.

But Jim Carrey loves playing against type. He thrives on surprising people both on and off camera. And playing a frightening stalker named Chip Douglas in *The Cable Guy* provided him with a chance to do just that.

Chapter 13

BIG CHANGES

IF NO ONE ELSE could figure out what had attracted Jim to *The Cable Guy*, or to the character of Chip Douglas, Jim was very clear about it. "I love the danger of him," Jim explained when the film was released in 1996. "You can never really figure this guy out. . . . I don't even know if I would call [the movie] dark. It's dark only in the sense that this is a disturbed needy person and we need to take that to the maximum level. We pump up the volume on that. But he's not really as disturbed as I am, normally. I had to bring it down for this."

Jim didn't see *The Cable Guy* as a heavy psychological thriller. In fact, there were parts he found downright funny. "There's something about this movie that's very strange and disquieting, and at the same time I've just fallen off my chair laughing. We're taking our premise to the maximum level. We've got this disturbed needy person and you never really know if he's just messin' with people or if he really does just need a friend."

Jim loved working with director Ben Stiller on the film. As a comedian who'd gone on to act and direct, Ben understood Jim's need to stretch himself. Ben let Jim experiment with the role of Chip Douglas and take his talent in new directions. Jim, in turn, appreciated Ben's support and directing style.

"I want to build a statue to Ben Stiller," Jim told one reporter. "I need a lot of room when I do a scene. Ben realizes this and knows just where to put the camera. He's truly amazing."

Unfortunately, that was probably the only time the word "amazing" was attached to *The Cable Guy*. Audiences were not nearly as fascinated as Jim was with the character of Chip Douglas, a cable repairman who becomes obsessed with an architect, stalking him in hope of forcing him to become his friend. Even the presence of the likable Matthew Broderick, as the tormented architect, did nothing to enhance the movie's box office appeal. In the end, *The Cable Guy* was relegated to cable itself, and Jim had to face his first failure in a very long time.

But Jim didn't seem concerned. His mind and his heart were elsewhere. When his divorce from Melissa became final, Jim and Lauren were married in a ceremony on a hillside near Malibu. The wedding, on September 23, 1996, was a quiet ceremony, with only a justice of the peace, Jim's brother John, and nine-year-old Jane in attendance.

Surprisingly, the press stayed away from the ceremony, probably because they were off chasing the late John F. Kennedy Jr. and his wife, Carolyn, who married the same weekend. Later, Jim and Lauren sent out a press statement. Lauren was excited about her "very sparkly" wedding ring. Jim added that, "despite the sometimes mind-boggling excitement I now face on a day-to-day basis I am striving to live a loving and honorable life."

Jim had little time to enjoy his newlywed status before he got busy on a new project. This one was closer to what his fans expected, a slapstick comedy called *Liar Liar*.

Jim relied on his talent for physical comedy to bring life to *Liar Liar*. He also brought in Tom Shadyac, the director who had started him on his road to success in *Ace Ventura, Pet Detective*.

The premise of *Liar Liar* is simple: Jim plays a fast-talking liar (and lawyer) who suddenly gets hit with a magic spell that prevents him from lying for one whole day.

"It could have been a one-joke movie, but with Jim we could take it in all sorts of directions," Tom Shadyac told *Entertainment Weekly*. "It's similar in tone to *Mrs. Doubtfire*. It's the movie that proves Jim can act in a human dramatic role but still deliver big laughs."

Audiences were thrilled to have the old Jim back. They greeted this new comedy with his largest ticket sales ever, excluding *Batman Forever*, which can't really be considered a Jim Carrey movie, since he had only a supporting role.

Once again Jim had scored big in a comedy hit. The time was obviously ripe for Jim to try his hand at an even bigger, wackier comedy . . . right?

Wrong. As expected, Jim did the unexpected. He took on a role he'd actually committed to two years before—in a serious drama called *The Truman Show*. Once again, all bets were off.

Chapter 14 ::

GOIN'
FOR THE GOLD

BY 1996, THE WORLD had taken voyeurism to a new level. MTV had a hit with *The Real World*, a show about a group of real-life twenty-somethings whose every move is captured by the cameras. The Internet had given people who were so inclined a means to broadcast their daily lives to the world—and people were tuning in to watch! *The Truman Show* was a science-fiction look at what would happen if people's desire to be Peeping Toms went too far.

In the movie Jim plays Truman Burbank, a doofy insurance salesman who lives with a perfect little wife in a perfect little house in a perfect little town. What Truman doesn't know is that all the people in his life are really actors and that his entire life is actually a hit TV show.

The role was a huge departure for Jim, and he was excited about the challenge. "It's not Shakespeare, but it's a more human character than anything I've ever

done. . . . It's like a Chaplin thing, with funny characters and whimsy and laughs. But it's got serious
undertones and issues."

Jim could totally relate to Truman's plight. Being a
celebrity, he often felt that the cameras were turned on
him at all times, too. "I've brought family pictures
to the Fotomat and had them end up in newspapers,
sold from the photo processing lab," Jim told
Entertainment Weekly. "People are, like, 'You can't
arrest me, you can't sue me, so just because you're
famous I'm going to make you feel like crap.' But I
never signed anything that said I wasn't a human
being anymore."

Jim and Lauren rented a mansion in Seaside,
Florida, while *The Truman Show* was in production.
By all accounts, the couple were happily in love.
Lauren visited the set while Jim was shooting scenes,
and she sometimes helped him learn his lines while he
skateboarded around the mansion's huge garage.
Lauren was by Jim's side for most of the shooting
schedule. But toward the end she had to leave to film a
movie of her own, *No Looking Back.*

It seemed innocent enough at the time, but only ten
months after Jim and Lauren had married, she filed for
divorce. While they would later attempt a reconcilia-
tion, their marriage was over.

Although Jim truly believed in *The Truman Show,*
he was concerned about how the film would be
received. The bad notices and poor fan reaction to *The
Cable Guy* still smarted. It was a gutsy move on his
part to take another departure from his comedic path.

And as Jim admitted to an AOL chat audience, going from goofball to dramatic actor wasn't an easy transition for him.

"The most difficult part of [making the transition from comedy to drama] is the idea that you become raw in a dramatic acting role. You have to open yourself up to the ultimate criticism. Whereas if you're funny they can say, 'The routine wasn't good' or 'I don't like his jokes.' But in a dramatic role it's more of 'I don't like that guy's essence.' "

Jim's fear of being universally trashed for his work in *The Truman Show* wasn't completely unfounded. His big price tag and high-profile success made him a target. And since the troubles with *The Cable Guy,* the press knew that more serious roles could be Jim's Achilles' heel.

Even Peter Weir, the movie's director, acknowledged that some of Jim's fans would stay away from *The Truman Show.* "We'll probably lose a certain number of Carrey fans. It's not for them. They'll be bored."

The pressure for success was fierce. But Jim faced the stress with characteristic good humor. "I guess I'll go into the fetal position for a few days," Jim joked to Oprah Winfrey when she asked what he would do if *The Truman Show* failed.

Luckily, Jim never had to curl up and pretend to return to the womb. Reviews for *The Truman Show* were wonderful. *Entertainment Weekly* called Jim's portrayal of Truman, "a bracingly grown-up performance that's winning raves and drawing comparisons to Tom Hanks's work in *Forrest Gump.*"

The combination of curiosity and Carrey brought fans to the movies in droves. *The Truman Show* earned $31 million in its very first weekend!

So now Jim had fame, fortune, and critical acclaim. What he didn't have was a gold statue on his mantel. But that was soon remedied. In March 1999 Jim won a Golden Globe award for his performance in *The Truman Show*.

Being acknowledged by the Hollywood foreign press was a huge honor for Jim. It was an acknowledgment of his work as an actor, not of his public persona as a "star." Being up on the stage, accepting a Golden Globe award for Best Dramatic Actor, was, in Jim's lingo, "a total joygasm!"

Usually the Golden Globes are a precursor to the Oscars. Winners of the Globes are at the very least on the list of Academy Award nominees. But the Academy passed over Jim. When the nominations were announced, Jim Carrey's name wasn't there.

Jim's fans and the press were shocked at the omission. But if Jim was disappointed, he didn't let on. Good sport that he is, Jim agreed to be a presenter on the Academy Awards show, although he made mention of the obvious oversight when he stepped out on the stage to make his presentation.

"I'm here to present the Academy Award for outstanding achievement for film editing. . . . That's all I'm here to do," he added slowly. Then he went on to say, "Winning the Oscar is not the most important thing in the world. It's an honor just to be nom . . . Oh, God!" At that point Jim burst into huge crocodile tears. The audience cracked up. Once again, Jim had used his humor to lighten a stressful situation.

After *The Truman Show,* one question was on everyone's mind: What would Jim Carrey do next? Was he going to become a serious actor, or would he go back to his comedic roots?

The answer was both. Although Jim did do a quick unbilled stint in the drama *Simon Birch,* his next big project was taking on the role of the late comedian Andy Kaufman in *Man on the Moon.* To Jim, playing Andy Kaufman, a real comedian's comedian, was serious business. It would take all of his energy to turn himself into a man Jim had admired for many years.

But to Andy's close friend and *Man on the Moon* producer Danny DeVito, Jim and Andy already had an awful lot in common. "Jim's always looking to clown around and do stuff like that," Danny told *People* Online. "The only difference is you see [the real] Jim. Andy you never saw. He was always on."

Andy Kaufman's brand of humor was certainly nothing like anything anyone had seen before or since. Although most people remember him as the foreign cabdriver on TV's *Taxi,* his stand-up comedy act had a much harder edge. Andy was known to evoke laughs—and revulsion—by coming onstage as Tony Clifton, a vulgar chauvinist, and refusing to break character.

Even when he was simply being Andy Kaufman, Andy could aggravate people. In one routine he worked with pro wrestler Jerry Lawler. Andy so infuriated Lawler that the wrestler actually tried to beat him up! Andy was putting him on, but Lawler didn't know that. It was hard to tell when Andy was pulling a gag on someone. In fact, because Andy was always putting people on, most of his friends didn't believe it when, in 1984, it was announced that Andy had died of a rare form of lung cancer. They figured it was another of Andy's jokes.

Jim focused all of his energy on becoming Andy Kaufman for *Man on the Moon*. Although Jim had never seen Andy perform live, he had seen him on TV and video. "I was a crazy fan, and as I went along I started getting these tapes and blurbs of things he had done," Jim told Dick Clark at the *2000 Golden Globe Awards Show*. "He was a gutsy dude who kinda went through the door and took all the flak. He opened things up for people like me."

Jim felt he owed Andy a performance that was true to the comedian's spirit. "It was very important for me to do justice to him," Jim says. "He was on such another level. He had a pure need to create. He was like Geppetto. He walked into a room and didn't see people who would like him or not like him, hurt him or help him. He saw the world as his own little puppet show. . . . I think of him as the Neil Armstrong of comedy. He went places no one else had gone."

So obsessed was Jim with paying tribute to Andy that he literally became the man while he was on the set, staying in character even between takes. He pulled Andy-like stunts, requesting two trailers—one for Andy and one for Tony Clifton. He rented an ice-cream truck and gave everyone on the set a snack—as long as they sang a song first. At one point Jim, remaining in character, offended the real Jerry Lawler (who had been hired to play himself in the film) after the cameras had stopped rolling. In a strange echo of Andy's real life, Jerry Lawler attacked Jim. At the time, Jim's manager, Eric Gold released a statement that "Mr. Lawler acted unprofessionally and attacked Jim Carrey. He attacked him and injured Jim's neck."

Even after production on *Man on the Moon* had ended, Jim continued to pull Andy-like stunts, coming to the MTV Movie Awards dressed as a look-alike for the late lead singer of the Doors, Jim Morrison. No one even realized it was Jim Carrey under the thick beard and long hair until he went up to the podium to receive his award for *The Truman Show!*

Jim was aware that his behavior was viewed as strange by some on the set, but he was determined to remain true to his gut instinct that in order to play Andy, he had to stay in character. As he puts it, "I'm not saying I had to go insane to do the film, but I know that there were some nights I went to bed as a character who was insane."

Jim's hard work paid off. Critics hailed his portrayal of Andy Kaufman. And although *Man on the Moon* was not the financial smash that Universal studios was hoping for, it did cement Jim's reputation as an actor to be reckoned with in Hollywood. Still, no one was as shocked as Jim was when he won the Golden Globe award as best actor in a comedy or musical for his portrayal of Andy Kaufman. After all, Jim had thought of *Man on the Moon* as a drama.

"Y'know, I was a little shocked that it was in the comedy or musical category," he admitted in his acceptance speech. "But y'know, I'll go with it. I'll get a songbook. Right to Broadway, man." Then he began to sing "You Can't Get a Man with a Gun," a song from *Annie Get Your Gun*, the popular musical. Obviously, the real Jim Carrey was back among us.

Sadly, once again, Jim's Golden Globe–winning performance was ignored by Oscar voters in 2000. Although Jim may have been disappointed at losing another shot at bringing home the statue, he was too busy to be overly concerned. When the names of the Oscar nominees were announced, he was putting the finishing touches on his next film, a wacky comedy called *Me, Myself and Irene*.

Me, Myself and Irene was definitely a return to the kind of comedy that had first raised Jim to superstar status. Once again he teamed up with the Farrelly brothers, who'd written and directed *Dumb & Dumber*. This time around, Bob and Peter were high on the success of their big hit *There's Something About Mary*. Originally the brothers had agreed to write the script for *Me, Myself and Irene* and leave the directing to somebody else. But when Jim decided to sign on to the project, the Farrelly brothers opted to direct the on-set madness themselves.

With *There's Something About Mary*, the Farrelly brothers had taken slapstick comedy to an extreme. *Me, Myself and Irene* took things even further, with sight gags involving animals (they were all animatronic, no animals were actually injured, honest), and an all-new set of butt jokes. Things were so gross and strange that people began to wonder whether there was *anything* Jim wouldn't do for a laugh.

"Y'know, I don't know where the line is yet," Jim admitted to E! Online. Then he acknowledged that he and the Farrelly brothers do share a decidedly bizarre sense of humor. Describing an average day on the set, he explained, "Typically, I'd go into the trailer for an hour or two . . . then come out and say, 'Okay. What sick, twisted fantasy would you like to vicariously live through me?'"

Jim loved the premise of *Me, Myself and Irene*—a man with two personalities, named Hank and Charlie, both of whom were in love with the same woman. "I really loved the concept of two schizophrenic entities falling in love with the same person. . . . I could play two characters in the film and have them play off each other," he explains. "It was a chance to go and do the careless thing a little bit. . . . Just have a good time."

Jim's female costar on the wild *Me, Myself and Irene* ride was Renee Zellweger, a beautiful actress best known for her work as Tom Cruise's love interest in *Jerry Maguire*. By all accounts Jim was smitten with Renee almost from the start. But unlike his on-screen *Dumb & Dumber* romance with Lauren Holly Jim hit a major roadblock with Renee while the movie was in production. Renee had a rule that she never dated anyone with whom she was working. She and Jim would hang out together, going for long walks along the shore of Lake Champlain. She also showed up with the rest of the cast at an ice-skating party Jim arranged at an indoor rink. But the only romance she allowed for was on-screen . . . until filming ended.

By the time *Me, Myself and Irene* was released in the summer of 2000, Jim and Renee were a full-fledged item. He visited her in London while she was working on the movie *Bridget Jones,* and they hung out together at her Los Angeles home, playing with her dog, Woof. Jim told reporters for *People* magazine that Renee was "absolutely a gem of a human being. She's very funny, even though she can be bashful at times." But he was careful not to reveal too much about the relationship to the press. He'd been burned before, and this relationship was far too important for him to risk any outside interference. No doubt about it, like Hank and Charlie, Jim Carrey had totally flipped for Renee.

Chapter 15

IT'S NOT EASY BEING GREEN

WHEN AUDREY GEISEL, widow of Dr. Seuss (his real name was Theodor Geisel) announced that she would allow producers to make a live-action movie based on one of her husband's most famous books, *How the Grinch Stole Christmas,* a bidding war broke out in Hollywood. It seemed that every studio wanted to bring the small-hearted meanie who steals Christmas from Whoville to the big screen.

Eventually, the rights went to Universal Studios in partnership with Imagine films. It was the joining with Imagine that sealed the deal, because Mrs. Geisel was a huge fan of Ron Howard, one of the founding partners of Imagine. She agreed that Universal could have the rights to *The Grinch* as long as Ron Howard directed the film.

Okay, so now *The Grinch* had a studio and a director. What it didn't have was a star. Not just anybody could play the Grinch. The actor who took on that role would have to have a truly devilish side in addition to being a long, lean physical comic. Now, who could that be?

Jim told E! Online that he was excited to have been cast in the role. "*Grinch* is a total honor to be part of," he remarked. "I felt like I won the lottery to be able to play the Grinch." Actually, Jim did better than the average lottery winner by signing on to the film. Universal agreed to pay his $20 million price tag and give him a piece of the merchandising rights.

But if Jim thought he was just going to have a good time doing another physical comedy, he was in for a real shock. *The Grinch* was hard work, especially for someone like Jim, who can't sit still. In fact, sitting patiently in the makeup chair may just have been the toughest part of playing the Grinch for Jim. Every morning at four-thirty he had to be on the set, ready to begin the transformation that turned him into the guy with "termites in his smile." Throughout the film, Jim was covered from head to toe in green makeup. And although Universal and Imagine preferred to keep Jim's Grinch look a secret until the film opened, word leaked out from the set that Jim was almost unrecognizable after the makeup folks had had their way with him.

While the makeup did turn Jim into the Grinch, it also provided him with a challenge. Jim realized that for the first time, really young kids would be seeing one of his movies. As a father, Jim was concerned that little children not be petrified at the sight of the Grinch. He kept that in mind while putting together his characterization of the Grinch.

"I didn't look at him like he's just an angry guy," Jim explained to E! Online. "What we are is hurt. Whether it's self-imposed or something happened to us, or whatever, we're hurt. And it manifests itself in anger. [Thinking of the Grinch in that way] enabled me to make him sympathetic, because it could've gotten scary with all that makeup and stuff, and kids are going to have to be able to watch it."

Jim finished filming *The Grinch* in the middle of 2000. Rumors flew about what project he would take on next. Some tabloids and Internet sites had Jim taking on a part in *The Incredible Mr. Limpet,* a remake of the old Don Knotts movie in which Mr. Limpet is granted a wish to become a fish. Plans were for Jim to play the title role in live action sequences. Animators would then create a fish that looked like Jim for the animated parts of the movie. Jim would do the voice for the talking fish. But there were clashes between Warner Brothers studio and the writers over the script, and eventually the project was postponed.

Another film Jim was rumored to be interested in pursuing was *Phone Booth,* the story of a man who answers a ringing pay phone and is told by a terrorist that he will be killed if he hangs up. Jim was attracted to *Phone Booth* partly because it was going to be directed by Joel Schumacher, who had directed Jim in *Batman Forever.* Jim also liked the idea behind the film.

"*Phone Booth* is an important story," he told E! Online. "Not only is it a great experiment—the film will be shot in two weeks, and the whole thing takes place in a phone booth—but the scope of the piece is important to me. . . . It's everything we have to deal with to get to a healthy place—our secrets and whatever mistakes we've made that we think are so bad." According to E! Online, Jim was also intrigued by the fact that Fox studios planned to show rehearsal footage from *Phone Booth* on the Internet so fans could see the details of how the movie was being made.

There were other scripts on Jim's short list as well. One of those was *Bijou,* a drama about a film writer who is placed on a professional blacklist by The House UnAmerican Activities Committee in 1951. When he arrives in a small town, the people there decide that he is the long-lost son of the owner of the local movie theater.

At the same time, Jim was also believed to have been considering trying his hand at yet another comedy, *The Scared Guys,* which was slated to be directed for Columbia Pictures by Dean Parisot (who also directed *The Crew*).

But by the end of the summer of 2000, Jim had not yet decided whether one of these scripts or a different film altogether would be his next project. So his fans had no idea whether Jim would to go for humor or angst in his next film.

Keeping folks guessing was just what Jim had in mind. "The very people who say 'I just want him to do this one thing that I like' will be the first people to get tired of you," Jim insists. "So you've got to zig and zag. You can't just give them what you think they want. My audience may be made fun of sometimes, but I believe they know there's more to me."

One project Jim was certain he would not be doing was the long-awaited sequel to *The Mask*. He told an AOL chat audience, "I'm not a crazy fan of going over old territory. And although *The Mask* was a great thing, I don't really plan on doing [the sequel]. You can never say never, but not really. I'm getting an opportunity to do all these new and wonderful things. Why waste my life being repetitive?"

Whatever Jim's next project will be, one thing is for sure, it will be completely different from anything else at the local movieplex. And it will probably be quite different from anything Jim Carrey has done before.

"I can't stay in one place for very long," he says of his career choices. He explained to Movieclub.com, "I am an explorer, and I need to discover new lands. Sometimes you have to dive into the abyss to get to another place. And I've never been afraid to dive into the abyss."

Luckily for Jim Carrey, his fans seem willing to follow him to whatever land he may explore next.

Chapter 16

Fast Facts

Everything You Need to Know about Jim Carrey

Full name: James Eugene Carrey. Jim hates his middle name, but he admits that it does have a purpose. "My parents gave me that [middle] name to keep me humble. You can't get too cool with a name like Eugene," he told *Tribute* magazine.

Childhood nicknames: Jimmy, Jimmy Gene the String Bean

Original family surname: Carré (The family is of French descent.)

Birthday: January 17, 1962

Zodiac sign: Capricorn with a moon in Gemini

Birthplace: Newmarket, Ontario, Canada

Eyes: Brown

Hair: Brown

Height: 6 feet 2 inches

Father: Percy Carrey, musician and accountant (deceased)

Mother: Kathleen (Kay), former singer (deceased)

Siblings: John, Pat, and Rita (all older)

Daughter: Jane Carrey, whose mother is Melissa Womer

Residence: Brentwood, California

Current girlfriend: Renee Zellweger

Morning or late night person: "I tend to stay up late, not because I'm partying but it's the only time of day when I'm alone and I don't have to be on, performing."

Favorite band: Phish. Jim actually arranged for a private Phish concert on June 24, 1999. The audience was the cast and crew of *Me, Myself and Irene*. Jim sang Pink Floyd's "Hey You" and the Beatles' "Come Together" with the band.

Favorite cartoon character: Deputy Dawg

Favorite snack: Potato chips and Häagen-Dazs ice cream

How Jim spends his free time: "Movies, movies, movies. I rent 'em and I go to see 'em all the time."

Favorite authors: Ayn Rand and C. S. Lewis. He also enjoys books about philosophy and metaphysical concepts.

What makes him laugh: "Someone who says something that makes absolutely no sense at all."

The best part of award-winning success: "It's nice to finally get scripts offered to me that aren't the ones Tom Hanks wipes his butt with!"

Surprising talents: Jim's a talented cartoonist and ventriloquist.

Present car: A vintage Thunderbird convertible

Chapter 17

LIGHTS, CAMERA, ACTION

MANY PEOPLE WERE SURPRISED that Jim Carrey was willing to take on serious roles in films like *The Cable Guy* and *The Truman Show*. They found it odd that someone so famous for comedy would try something completely different.

But were those roles really such a change from characters Jim had played in the past? All true Jim Carrey fans know that the answer to that question is "Absolutely not." Throughout his career, Jim has played a whole slew of different types of characters. Some were serious, some were dangerous, and some were just butt-talking nuts. But a common thread ran through all of them: they all had a distinctly human and real side.

To get a handle on Jim Carrey's diverse talents, you've got to study his career from the very beginning. You can start by reading this chapter, and then heading over to your local video store to check out some Jim Carrey videos. But be warned that once you start on a Jim Carrey movie marathon, it's tough to stop. Jim's movies are like potato chips—you can't have just one. And since Jim's career is now into its third decade, you could spend a lot of time in front of that VCR.

Introducing Janet: This dramatic film was first broadcast on Canadian television in September 1981. The movie tells the story of two teens who become friendly and help each other discover their hidden talents.

Jim plays Tony Maroni, a really bad stand-up comic—how's that for irony? Actually, the casting doesn't seem so strange when you realize that it takes a really good comic to know how to throw his timing off just enough to make an act not work. If you're at the video store looking for *Introducing Janet,* you'll never find it. The film was later retitled *Rubber Face,* in an attempt to cash in on Jim's comedic fame.

Copper Mountain: Made in 1982 for the CTV network, this was Jim's second TV movie. But unlike *Introducing Janet,* which concerns a friendship between two teens, there is nothing serious about this combo of sports, rock and roll, and sex appeal.

Copper Mountain takes place at a Club Med ski resort. Playing Bob, a guy with a weird nervous tic that has him doing impressions whenever he gets stressed out, allows Jim to take his comedy act to the small screen. In this movie he performs in a way that is more Jim Carrey than he was able to do in *Introducing Janet*.

Copper Mountain is certainly not memorable. In fact, the low-budget flick is no longer even available on video. Considering it's a Jim Carrey movie, that says a lot.

All in Good Taste: This small Canadian film was actually in production in 1980—before Jim appeared in *Introducing Janet*—but it wasn't released until 1983. It's actually unfair to call this a Jim Carrey film. After all, Jim had no lines and very little screen time in this story about a screenwriter who discovers that his wholesome script about an orphan and a dog has been turned into a risqué movie about strippers. It's tough to find *All in Good Taste* anymore—although some Internet users have claimed to have discovered copies hidden in their video stores.

Finders Keepers: Richard Lester, the man behind the classic Beatles films *A Hard Day's Night* and *Help!*, directed this wacky 1984 chase movie which starred Beverly D'Angelo, Louis Gossett Jr., and Michael O'Keefe. The comedy had it all—stolen money, disguises, con artists, and chase scenes on a train. When Jim took on the small part of Lane Bidlekoff in the film he was sure he was in yet another of Richard Lester's comic classics. No such luck. As movie reviewer Leonard Maltin put it, the movie "remains disappointingly flat." Audiences agreed, and before long, *Finders Keepers* disappeared from view—though you can find it at your video store.

Once Bitten: Model-turned-actress Lauren Hutton is the Countess, a Hollywood vampire in search of the blood of a male virgin. If she doesn't find it soon, she'll begin to look her actual age—about 400! Guess who winds up supplying her with what she needs?

Once Bitten didn't give Jim much of a chance to show off his stuff. Still, he did what he could with the part, including a three-legged dance routine that's completely off the wall. As Film.Com puts it, "Carrey uses a lot of physical energy to make up for the fact that he doesn't have a character to play."

Once Bitten was not a huge hit, but it did turn a profit. And of course, in video it has become somewhat of a success, specifically because Jim's fans view the film as part of his history.

Peggy Sue Got Married: *Peggy Sue Got Married* is best remembered for the performances of Kathleen Turner and Nicolas Cage, who played the leads in this romantic comedy directed by Francis Ford Coppola. (Small world alert: Francis Ford Coppola is actually Nicolas Cage's uncle. Nicolas is one of Jim's good friends.) As Charlie's buddy, Walter Getz, Jim's screen time is so short you might miss him if you blink. But there is one scene that you can fast forward to if you're in search of classic Carrey. Find the spot where Nicolas and Jim perform as part of a doo-wop quintet.

There were no mentions of Jim's small performance in the original reviews of the movie, but once he became famous, video reviewers were sure to remind fans to keep an eye out for Jim's portrayal of the high school best friend who grows up to be a drug-snorting dentist.

Peggy Sue Got Married was one of the hits of 1986, earning more than $40 million at the box office. Today you can catch it playing on cable TV on a regular basis.

The Dead Pool: *The Dead Pool* was Clint Eastwood's fifth and final turn as Dirty Harry Callahan, perhaps his most popular on-screen persona. In this flick, a weird betting game is being played: people are gambling on which celebrity will be the next to die. Clint handpicked Jim for the part of Johnny Shakes, a wacky drug-addicted rock singer who's the first celeb to bite the dust.

A Dirty Harry movie release was an event back in 1988. The film opened to nice reviews. Even the notorious curmudgeon Roger Ebert praised the film, saying, "It knows who Dirty Harry is and how we react to him, and it has fun with its intelligence."

Although critics didn't mention Jim by name, his role in the movie gave him great exposure. And since Clint Eastwood had given him permission to be as wacky as he wanted, the audience truly got to see the real Jim Carrey—actually the real James Carrey, which is the way Jim is listed in the credits.

Pink Cadillac: Jim had a small role in this Clint Eastwood movie—his character was credited simply as Lounge Singer—but he didn't mind. Any chance to share the screen with Clint was a thrill for Jim. In this case he got to pull out his old Elvis imitation and perform it on the silver screen. You'll find Jim shaking his hips onstage in the nightclub scene, singing "Blue Suede Shoes." The spotlight in that scene is on Clint and Broadway actress Bernadette Peters. Jim just provides the ambience.

In this movie, Clint plays a bounty hunter who's trying to nab a bail jumper named Roy who has run off with his neo-Nazi buddies and taken his baby with him. Clint agrees to help Roy's wife Lou Ann (Bernadette Peters) get her baby back.

Reviews for the movie were mixed. *Washington Post* reviewer Hal Hinson summed up the general view of the film by calling *Pink Cadillac* "Embraceable movie trash that seduces you into dropping your defenses. It's weightlessly, undeniably, enjoyable."

What more can you ask for?

Earth Girls Are Easy: Finally, Jim Carrey finds a movie where he can totally be himself—an alien from outer space. It's hard to describe *Earth Girls Are Easy*—it's kind of a sci-fi romantic musical comedy. Think of it as an alien-invasion flick for the MTV generation. Its a mishmash for sure, but somehow the film works, mostly thanks to the amazing talent of the cast. The movie stars Jeff Goldblum, Damon Wayans, and Jim Carrey as aliens whose spaceship splashes down in Geena Davis's pool. Sometimes it's hard to tell who's weirder—the aliens or the Valley girls they meet up with.

Earth Girls Are Easy had a rocky beginning—it was originally supposed to be released in 1988 but it was put on a shelf until 1989, when it premiered at the Toronto International Film Festival. Eventually the movie opened nationwide—and audiences loved it. Critic Leonard Maltin called the film an "Infectiously goofy musical comedy."

High Strung: In this bizarre 1991 comedy, Jim takes on one of the most ominous characters of his career—Death. *High Strung* stars Steve Oederek—who later went on to write *Ace Ventura: When Nature Calls*—as a cranky children's book author who does nothing but complain. He hates everything, including pets, insects, his neighbors, even watermelon-flavored Popsicles. Then one day he begins to receive strange phone calls, warning him that something is going to happen at eight o'clock that night. Jim's name doesn't appear in the credits of this film (he did it as a favor to his bud, Steve), but his presence is definitely felt. This movie is available on video, but it can be tough to find.

Doing Time on Maple Drive: Talk about a serious movie. There's nothing funny about life on Maple Drive. In fact life there is incredibly sad. Jim's role as Tim, the alcoholic son of a demanding and unrelenting father, was a complete departure from his goofball work in *Earth Girls Are Easy*. Jim took this part very seriously. The result was a mesmerizing performance that will go down as one of Jim's most memorable.

The movie aired on the Fox television network on March 16, 1992. It enjoyed high ratings, and earned three Emmy nominations. Although Jim wasn't one of the nominees, he did receive good reviews for his work. Today you can catch rebroadcasts of the movie from time to time on Lifetime.

Ace Ventura, Pet Detective: This wacky 1994 comedy is widely considered Jim's breakout film. Nobody could've predicted it at the time, since *Ace Ventura* was a small film with a mere $15 million budget. When the movie first came out, the reviews were beyond bad. *Washington Post* reviewer Desson Howe called *Ace Ventura, Pet Detective*, "a mindless stretch of nonsense." And Roger Ebert warned his readers that he "found the movie a long, unfunny slog through an impenetrable plot."

Despite such warnings, this story of of a Florida gumshoe who cracks cases involving animals became a comedy classic. Fans couldn't get enough of Jim's wackiness as his character, Ace, goes out in search of a football team's mascot. Before anyone knew it, Jim Carrey was a household name, and kids everywhere were trying to talk through their butts and shouting out "All righty then!" Cash registers at movie theaters bulged nationwide as the film earned $12 million in its first week and eventually went on to gross $72 million in its initial release.

The Mask: Jim had two roles in this totally whacked-out comedy—as a wormy bank teller who becomes a fearless green-faced, wacky wild man every time he places an old wooden Viking mask on his face. Playing two different roles in one man provided a showcase for Jim's acting prowess and crazy cartoon-like antics. Whenever he came on the screen in his bright yellow suit and huge hat, audiences couldn't be sure what insanity might ensue.

The animation for *The Mask* was flawless, thanks to the special effects wizards at Industrial Light and Magic. Working within the film's $20 million budget, they created a world in which the line between reality and cartoon was seamless.

The Mask earned a phenomenal $120 million in the United States alone. As the Mask would say, "Somebody stop me!"

Dumb & Dumber: This is a road trip buddy movie, Jim Carrey style. In this flagrantly funny flick, Jim (playing limo driver Lloyd Christmas) and costar Jeff Daniels (playing Lloyd's friend Harry) take to the road and travel halfway across the country to return a briefcase to a beautiful passenger who left it in Lloyd's car.

By the movie's 1994 release, critics were used to Jim's antics, and they were able to see Jim's frenetic comedic style for the true art form that it is. The reviews for *Dumb & Dumber* matched the enthusiasm of the fans. The *San Francisco Chronicle* called it "a smart comedy with lowbrow laughs" and went on to describe the film as an "inspired, irreverent, spark-driven comedy that takes you places you never thought a movie would go—even a Jim Carrey movie!"

In their *Video Movie Guide* Mick Martin and Marsha Porter say that Jim and Jeff were "to the 1990s what Laurel and Hardy were to the 1930s and Abbott and Costello were to the 1940s." High praise for the king of lowbrow comedy and his cohort.

Dumb & Dumber proved that Jim's previous successes were no fluke. The film earned $127 million in its initial 1994 U.S. release.

Batman Forever: It's rare for a leading actor to take on a supporting role after a string of huge successes, but who could blame Jim for wanting to play the Riddler in the third Batman movie? The Riddler was the perfect role for Jim. It required almost manic energy and an ability to practically dance across the screen as a comic book character brought to life.

Batman Forever was Jim's biggest budget film—it cost more than $100 million. Although all of the stars—Val Kilmer as Batman, Tommy Lee Jones as Two-Face, and Jim—earned hefty salaries, most of the cash went into the incredible special effects.

Batman Forever opened in the summer of 1995 on four thousand screens nationwide, a record at the time. It went on to earn more than $184 million in the United States—not as much as the original 1989 *Batman,* which starred Jack Nicholson as the Joker and Michael Keaton as the Caped Crusader, but more than 1992's *Batman Returns.*

Ace Ventura: When Nature Calls: This sequel to *Ace Ventura, Pet Detective* was an unusual career move for Jim. It's the only sequel he has ever agreed to do.

The premise was simple: Ace Ventura goes off to Africa to find a white bat. The comedy was classic Carrey. No animal joke was beneath him, whether it was taking a frightening ride on an ostrich, feeding an eagle mouth to mouth, or giving a mighty Tarzan yell through his rear end.

Reviews for *Ace Ventura: When Nature Calls* were even worse than those for the original Ace flick. *USA Today* said, "No doubt *Ace 2* will further engorge [Jim Carrey's] bank account. If only the jokes held more interest." And *Time* magazine added to the catcalls, insisting that *When Nature Calls* was "wearying, stupefying, and dumber than dumb."

Once again, however, Jim's fans proved immune to the critics' barbs. They packed the theaters. Eventually *Ace Ventura: When Nature Calls* earned $108 million, even more than the original!

The Cable Guy: When Jim took on the role of Chip Douglas, the frighteningly bizarre cable installer and repairman who stalks a mild-mannered architect in this dark 1996 film, he was obviously looking for a change after playing so many wildly comedic roles. Unfortunately, Jim's audiences couldn't connect with their favorite funnyman playing an obsessive, frightening character who was only occasionally humorous. Jim's fans stayed away from the film.

Still *The Cable Guy* did manage to earn $60 million in its initial release. That would have been a respectable figure for just about any movie. But not for a Jim Carrey starrer. As far as Hollywood was concerned, *The Cable Guy* was a flop.

Ironically, while the fans stayed away, the critics were kinder to *The Cable Guy* than they had been to *Ace Ventura: When Nature Calls*. Richard Schickel, for example, said that the movie's dark theme "suits Jim Carrey's comic genius with its eerie blend of sublime self-confidence and anarchical menace. . . . Like Matthew Broderick, as the customer watching this performance, fearful and fascinated, we have no choice but to let him into our lives." *USA Today* praised the casting of the movie, "Instead of boogers and belches *Guy* offers its star a comic foil of equal weight (the effectively mortified Matthew Broderick) and a more linear story than we've seen in the gag-happy vehicles that have thus typified Carrey's screen career." The *USA Today* review went on to praise Jim's hair-raising performance, saying that, "Carrey's lisping cable installer is frightening to both the eye and the brain. . . . Even at its worst, *The Cable Guy* is a legitimate curio."

Liar Liar: No lying—*Liar Liar* put Jim Carrey back at the top of the box office charts. The movie earned $181 million, almost as much as *Batman Forever*, with Jim as the sole big bankable star. The movie was a return to Jim's famous physical comedy shtick, but there was more to *Liar Liar* than gross jokes and toilet talk, although Jim did spend one scene bashing himself in the head with a toilet seat. Besides Jim's high-energy comedy, there seemed to be a real heart behind his performance as Fletcher Reid, a fast-talking attorney who also happens to be a perpetual liar. Fletcher really loves his five-year-old-son, even though the kid did wish for him to stop lying for twenty-four hours.

Audiences and critics alike cheered Jim's performance in *Liar Liar*. Even hard-to-please Roger Ebert admitted to becoming a fan of Jim's, calling the movie "a high-energy comeback" after *The Cable Guy,* and praising Jim by saying, "I can imagine the idea [of a lawyer forced to tell the truth] as getting old really fast with a lesser actor, but Carrey literally throws himself into the story."

HBO Online offered even higher praise, telling readers that "Jim Carrey shows the world how to turn a routine sitcom plot into a phenomenal box office hit."

The Truman Show: After the amazing reception of *Liar Liar,* Jim once again made a daring career move by taking on the title role of Truman Burbank, a man who lives in an idyllic small town, not realizing that he is the star of a reality-TV show about his own life. Andrew Niccol's script was smart and shrewd, and attracted Jim's love of the theater of the absurd.

Jim's performance in *The Truman Show* was a tour de force that critics unanimously adored. Mick Martin and Marsha Porter, in their *Video Movie Guide,* wrote of the "frankly astonishing performance from Jim Carrey that's leagues beyond anything he's ever done." Owen Gleiberman called *The Truman Show* "A beautifully sinister and transfixing entertainment-age daydream. . . . Carrey turns Truman into a postmodern Capra hero." And in Jim's hometown, Toronto.com praised his work, saying that his "performance as a hollow, grown-up child, surrounded by slavish actors looking for their own fifteen minutes is tinged with slivers of grisly tragedy."

The Truman Show gave Jim his first Golden Globe award. It also proved that he could bring in big money at the box office while taking on more challenging roles. The film delivered a whopping $125 million in its initial 1998 U.S. theater release.

Simon Birch: If *The Cable Guy* and *The Truman Show* were departures for Jim, being part of the cast of 1998's *Simon Birch* was totally off the wall. *Simon Birch* is one of those tug-at-your-heart-strings movies you'd never associate with someone who's been nick-named Rubberface. It is the story of a disabled boy who is trying to figure out his purpose on earth. Along the way he helps his friend Joe discover the identity of his real dad.

Many of the people who went to see *Simon Birch* were probably unaware that Jim had taken part in the movie. He appeared in only the first and last scenes, spending the rest of the time as an unseen narrator. Although he performed without billing, his work didn't escape the notice of the critics—and it didn't go over too well with them. Mike Clark of *USA Today* was especially unkind. He blasted Jim by writing that

"Carrey's dreadful narration as the grown-up Joe Mazzello pegs this as the kind of artistic lapse Billy Crystal and Robin Williams have been known to make when they want to be loved and not laughed at."

Ouch!

Man on the Moon: When word went out that casting was beginning on a film about comic Andy Kaufman, Jim was determined to get the role. He even agreed to audition for the part—a rarity for stars of his magnitude. When Jim was finally cast as Andy, he threw himself into the role, literally becoming Andy whenever he was on the set. The result was a phenomenally accurate portrayal of the comic.

It's not easy to play a real person, especially someone who lived recently and is remembered by a great number of people. But Jim was so like Andy on screen that the line between art and reality often seemed blurred. The movie re-created many of the most famous moments in Andy's life practically word for word. In fact, the entire cast of *Taxi*, the 1970s TV series that Andy once starred in, reunited to play themselves in the film.

The people who knew Andy best had high praise for Jim's portrayal of their pal. The critics followed in kind. *Movie Review International*'s Heather Clisby remarked that Jim "successfully slipped into Andy's skin with some ease, and it's a snug fit . . . the transformation is complete." *Entertainment Weekly*'s Owen Gleiberman agreed, saying that "Jim Carrey's performance is an impersonation on the level of genius."

But all the praise and Jim's *Golden Globe* weren't

enough to bring in the fans. The picture grossed only a mere $34 million before going into video release.

Me, Myself and Irene: There have always been two sides to Jim Carrey—the class clown and the sensitive soul. So it was only natural that he'd be drawn to the multiple-personality role of Charlie and Hank—two guys in one body. Charlie's a sweetie, sensitive and even a little nerdy. Hank's a creep, who's capable of just about anything if it means landing a lady. Both guys are in love with the same girl. Sounds like something only the Farrelly brothers could come up with. And it's a part only Jim Carrey could pull off.

When *Me, Myself and Irene* came out in the summer of 2000, the reviews were mixed. *Time* magazine's Richard Corliss felt that "Jim Carrey is twice as funny half the time," explaining that, as a moviegoer, you would "laugh your ass off in the first half of the movie . . . but the comedy needs a climax. And long before that *Me, Myself and Irene* goes slack and desperate." Still, Corliss did single out Jim's performance. "For his first real comedy in three years, Carrey is all manic ingenuity. His eyebrows tango, he sports a dry mouth and a milk mustache, he executes a quintuple spit take. . . . He has the timing and gall—as in his metamorphosis from Charlie to Hank in one shot and with no special effects. You don't need ILM when you have JIM."

The Grinch: By the end of the twentieth century, all the Whos down in Whoville—and folks in Hollywood as well—were wondering if Jim Carrey would agree to play Dr. Seuss's green-faced meanie in the movie version of *How the Grinch Stole Christmas*. He accepted the part in 1999 and was in front of the cameras by 2000.

There was no doubt in anyone's mind that the November 2000 release would be a huge success. As early as July 2000, *Entertainment Weekly* was predicting that "It's a no-brainer that this will be a big hit." Industry insiders predicted that the picture's gross would be at least $85 million, if not more, when all was said and done. And that was without any footage ever being shown. Toy companies were also betting big on a Grinchy Christmas, creating everything from computer games to action figures based on Jim's portrayal of the classic Dr. Seuss character.

Chapter 18

THE ENVELOPE, PLEASE

"I DON'T IMAGINE MYSELF winning things. I just work. That's the bottom line. That's what I love to do. I did not expect it." Jim was totally sincere when he made that declaration to a chat room audience after winning a Golden Globe for *The Truman Show* in 1999. He truly was shocked. "I was freaking out," he admitted. "Lauren Bacall opened the envelope up and all I heard was J . . . My brain went out the window. It was really great!"

Of course, Jim's fans were disappointed a few weeks later when he failed to be nominated for an Academy Award for his work in *The Truman Show*. But if Jim was upset by the slight, he certainly didn't show it. He was just happy for the film's success. Having his fans accept him in a drama was more important to him than all the trophies in the world. Jim really doesn't care about the awards, no matter how many fake tears he shed on the Academy Awards show.

But that hasn't stopped the folks who give out awards from sending a few statues Jim's way. While the Oscar has been elusive, there are plenty of trophies on Jim's mantelpiece. Here's a list of them.

Blockbuster Entertainment Awards

1995   Favorite Actor, Comedy, on Video—for *Ace Ventura, Pet Detective*

1995   Favorite Male Newcomer on Video—for *Ace Ventura, Pet Detective*

1998   Favorite Actor, Comedy—for *Liar Liar*

Boston Society of Film Critics Awards

1999   Best Actor—for *Man on the Moon*

Golden Globes

1999   Best Performance by an actor in a Motion Picture, Drama—for *The Truman Show*

2000   Best Performance by an actor in a Motion Picture, Comedy or Musical—for *Man on the Moon*

MTV Movie Awards

1995   Best Comedic Performance—for *Dumb & Dumber*

Best Kiss—for *Dumb & Dumber* (shared with Lauren Holly)

1996   Best Comedic Performance—for *Ace Ventura: When Nature Calls*

Best Male Performance—for *Ace Ventura: When Nature Calls*

1997 Best Comedic Performance—for *The Cable Guy*

Best Villain—for *The Cable Guy*

1998 Best Comedic Performance—for *Liar Liar*

1999 Best Male Performance—for *The Truman Show*

ShowWest Convention USA

2000 Male Star of the Year

Walk of Fame

2000 Star on the Hollywood Walk of Fame

Chapter 19

THE LEADER OF THE PACK

THERE'S NEVER BEEN AN actor quite like Jim Carrey. After all, while promoting *Ace Ventura, Pet Detective,* Jim himself said that "before *Ace Ventura,* no actor had considered talking through his ass."

But since *Ace Ventura,* lots of actors have been making butt jokes, fat jokes, sex jokes, and urinating jokes, though not always with the unique style Jim has displayed. The truth is, Jim Carrey has led a Hollywood revolution—an all-out gross-out slapstick attack on the film industry. Jim's influence can be seen in the work of many young comedic performers as well as having paved the way for some of his contemporaries:

Ben Stiller

Ben Stiller is the son of two famous comedians, Anne Meara and Jerry Stiller. His parents are comedy royalty. Besides having a great stand-up act, Anne has appeared in several movies and TV shows, including *Archie Bunker's Place*. Jerry is best remembered these days for having played George's loud, loud, *loud* father on *Seinfeld*. But even with that kind of legacy, Ben Stiller is truly a comedian in his own right.

Ben's connections to Jim run deep. For starters, like Jim, Ben first came to the attention of a national audience on a TV show that ran on the Fox network. *The Ben Stiller Show,* a comedy variety show, lasted less than a season in 1992, but it was enough time for audiences to learn to love Ben's offbeat sense of humor and his ability to take on several different characters. (Sound familiar?)

The personal connection began when Ben directed Jim in *The Cable Guy*. Ben later followed in Jim's footsteps by finding on-screen success in a Farrelly brothers movie, *There's Something About Mary*. In that movie Ben took big comedic risks: He battled with his zipper—and lost. Then he fought a wild terrier—and lost again. Just like Jim in *Dumb & Dumber,* Ben was able to remain so likable throughout *Something About Mary* that audiences cheered when he finally got the girl.

After *Something About Mary,* Ben followed Jim's lead by taking on different kinds of parts, always keeping the audience guessing as to what his next move would be. His most visible role came in 2000, in the religious comedy *Keeping the Faith,* in which he played a rabbi whose mother and congregation wanted to marry him off.

Many casting directors have noticed Jim's influence on Ben. This was never more true than in the case of Ben's latest pic, *Meet the Parents*. Ben is the man you see on screen as male nurse Greg Focker, but the role was originally offered to Jim. Ben says it was easy for him to tell the script was originally written for Jim. "The first draft I read must've been from when they were thinking of Jim because it was very physically oriented," Ben recalled in *Entertainment Weekly.* "Like the toilet's overflowing and my character sits on top to stop it. He uses himself as a human plug."

Mike Meyers

Call it the Canadian connection. Like Jim, *Saturday Night Live* alum Mike Myers hails from the north country. Mike's hometown is Scarborough, Ontario. Also like Jim, Mike says that his dad fostered his love of comedy. Mr. Myers would wake Mike up at night to watch old *Monty Python's Flying Circus* routines on TV.

Mike got interested in showbiz early. He was working professionally by the age of eight, doing commercials for Pepsi and Kit Kat candy bars. Eventually Mike's comedic talent helped him win a spot in Canada's Second City comedy troupe.

Mike came to the attention of folks in the States as a member of the cast of *Saturday Night Live* from 1989 to 1994. Almost from the beginning, Mike's ability to create and sustain characters—like Wayne, the host of "Wayne's World," and Dieter the German talk show host—made him a standout in the cast. Like

Jim, Mike has a unique ability to recall the things that made him laugh when he was a teenage boy—does anyone remember "schwing"?—and a lack of inhibitions when it comes to bringing those memories back to life.

Mike's comedic talent is probably best seen in *Austin Powers: International Man of Mystery* and *Austin Powers: The Spy Who Shagged Me,* in which Mike plays off-the-wall characters like Dr. Evil, Fat Bastard, and Austin Powers with classic slapstick (and incredibly gross) craziness. Madonna jokingly thanked Mike for his "sick" sense of humor when she accepted an MTV Music award for the video "Beautiful Stranger." The video featured Madonna and Mike, in his Austin Powers getup, performing some moves in a car.

Mike's next planned project is an undetermined film to be produced with Dreamworks SKG, Imagine Films, and Universal Studios.

Adam Sandler

Adam Sandler is another *Saturday Night Live* alumnus. Like Jim, Adam got his start in stand-up comedy. In fact, he was doing his act in Boston when he came to the attention of Dennis Miller, who was doing the "Weekend Update" news routine on *Saturday Night Live* at the time.

Besides being a featured performer, Adam quickly developed a reputation as a writer at *Saturday Night Live.* He took great pains to keep his characters fresh and funny. He wasn't above doing gross-out or dirty jokes—anything to get the audience laughing. After all, that's the whole point of being a comic.

Adam borrowed a lot from his stand-up routine for *Saturday Night Live.* His act often included strange song lyrics, which Adam sang in a flat monotone. His hysterical "Hanukkah Song," in which he names all the Jewish entertainers he can think of, has become a holiday classic. Never let it be said that Adam Sandler has ever been particularly politically correct. What fun is that?

Adam's first film, *Billy Madison,* set him off on a career that mirrored Jim's early days. The critics found the humor juvenile and totally dissed the film, but audiences ignored the critics. Adam went on to even bigger movie success with *Happy Gilmore, The Wedding Singer, The Waterboy,* and *Big Daddy.* Although he's never won the kind of critical acclaim that Jim finally achieved, industry insiders admit that Adam is a force to be reckoned with. His next release, *Little Nicky,* is almost universally predicted to be a huge hit. It stars Adam as a guy who's been asked by his dad to go into the family business, which would be all right, except that his dad is the devil. And in case you were in doubt about just how much influence Jim's life has had on Adam, consider this: Jim's old pal and mentor, Rodney Dangerfield, plays Adam's grandfather in the movie.

Jason Biggs

Jason is probably the youngest of today's comedians to follow in Jim's footsteps. He's sixteen years younger than Jim, so Jason is one of today's top comic actors who might have grown up watching Jim Carrey's movies. And it shows. Jason's most famous scene to date—his romance with an apple pie in the teen comedy *American Pie* is a Carrey-worthy performance if ever there was one.

Although gross-out comedy is definitely his forte, Jason didn't find his way into the comic world in a traditional manner. In fact, he started out playing it straight on the Broadway stage. His first role was in the serious play, *Conversations with My Father,* opposite Judd Hirsch. He then appeared in a soap opera, *As the World Turns.* Jason finally got to lighten up a little bit in the short-lived sitcom, *Drexell's Class.*

Since his *American Pie* days, Jason has gone on to film stardom, acting opposite Freddie Prinze Jr. and taking on the title role in the summer 2000 Amy Heckerling flick, *Loser.* In that movie, Jason wears a doofy hat and an even doofier expression on his face. It would be a direct take on *Dumb & Dumber,* except that Jason's character, Paul Tannek, is really smart. Jason's performance in the film is a comic tour de force that Jim Carrey would be proud of.

Next up for Jason? *Prozac Nation,* starring Christina Ricci, and the title role in 2001's *Saving Silverman.* Also look for *American Pie 2* in 2001.

Chapter 20

THE GREAT JIM CARREY QUIZ

OKAY, SO JUST HOW much do you know about the man behind *The Mask*'s mask? You can find out just how much Jim Carrey trivia is stored up in your brain by taking this quiz. Some of the questions may take a little (Pet) detective work as you search the pages of this book for the answers. Others are tougher than the Riddler's riddles—only Jim's biggest fans (and Jim himself, of course) will get them right.

No matter how tough the questions seem to you, you can be sure to find the right answers on pages 106–07. (Honest, the answers are there. You wouldn't call us a Liar Liar, wouldya?)

1. Name the first comedy club Jim ever performed in.
2. Who is Wiploc?
3. *The Dead Pool,* which featured Jim as Johnny

Shakes, was which of Clint Eastwood's Dirty Harry films?

a. third   b. fifth   c. seventh

4. The Cable Guy likes to call himself Chip Douglas. The name is a reference to the middle child on what TV show?

5. What is the name of the fictional cartoon show on *The Duck Factory?*

6. Who is Jane Carrey?
   a. Jim's mom b. Jim's first wife c. Jim's daughter

7. True or false: Due to all of the special effects, *The Mask* cost $75 million to make.

8. Name the screaming comic who was Jim's mentor during his Los Angeles comedy club days.

9. Jim dated which famous rock star of the 1970s?

10. What is the Mask's given name?

11. Finish the name of the TV movie Jim starred in: *Doing Time On* _____

12. *In Living Color* ran on what network?

13. On which soap opera did Lauren Holly appear?

14. Who is Ed Nygma?

15. The catchphrase "All righty then" first appeared in which of Jim's movies?
    a. *Ace Ventura, Pet Detective* b. *Dumb & Dumber* c. *The Mask*

16. In which movie did Jim play a limo driver named Lloyd Christmas?

17. Which cartoon character's theme song did Andy Kaufman perform in his act?

18. Which of Jim's characters lives in Edge City?

19. Name the L.A. Comedy Club owned by Mitzi

Shore where Jim often performed in the early 1980s.

20. *Ace Ventura: When Nature Calls* is supposedly set in Africa. Where was it actually filmed?
    a. Africa   b. Los Angeles   c. Texas

21. Who originally had the role of the evil director (later played by Ed Harris) in *The Truman Show?*

22. What 1941 Bob Hope film was the inspiration for *Liar Liar?*
    a. *To Tell the Truth*   b. *Nothing but the Truth*
    c. *Road to Morocco*

23. The cry "Somebody stop me!" was first heard in which of Jim's movies?
    a. *Batman Forever*   b. *The Mask*   c. *Liar Liar*

24. In *Me, Myself and Irene,* what is the name of the nice guy cop personality, Hank or Charlie?

25. What color was the tuxedo jacket Jim wore to the premiere of *Ace Ventura: When Nature Calls?*

26. What wish does Max make in *Liar Liar?*

27. Which team of brothers did Jim collaborate with on *Dumb & Dumber* and *Me, Myself and Irene?*

28. Jim played the best friend of his real-life buddy Nicolas Cage in what movie?

29. Which of Jim's characters has been described as a "nasty wasty skunk" with a heart three sizes too small?

30. Where did Jim get the idea for the Claw scene in *Liar Liar?*

Answers to the Great Jim Carrey Quiz

1. The Yuk Yuk Komedy Kabaret
2. Jim's character, also known as Alien #2, in *Earth Girls Are Easy*
3. b
4. *My Three Sons*
5. "Dippy Duck"
6. c
7. False. It only cost $20 million to make, a low figure, considering all of the effects.
8. Sam Kinison
9. Linda Ronstadt
10. Stanley Ipkiss
11. *Maple Drive*
12. Fox
13. *All My Children*
14. That is the alias of the Riddler in *Batman Forever.*
15. a
16. *Dumb & Dumber*
17. Mighty Mouse
18. The Mask
19. The Comedy Store
20. c
21. Dennis Hopper
22. b
23. b
24. Charlie
25. Crimson
26. That his dad will tell the truth for one full day
27. Peter and Bobby Farrelly

28. *Peggy Sue Got Married*
29. The Grinch
30. From a joke Percy Carrey used to play on his children and grandchildren

How Do You Rate:

25–30 correct: Wow! You're smokin'!

15–24 correct: All righty then. This is a pretty good score.

8–14 correct: Uh-oh! The Grinch has obviously stolen your VCR. You need to get it back and rent some Jim Carrey movies right away!

0–7 correct: It seems that the Cable Guy has cut off your access to the outside world. But you can catch up. Reread this book immediately!

Chapter 21

KEEPING JIM IN SITE

THE GRINCH IS COMING! And that means Jim will have to go out on a major publicity blitz. He's already made his first *Grinch* pitch . . . on the September 2000 MTV Video Music Awards. Pretty soon his grinning face—green or otherwise—is going to be everywhere! So how can you be sure that you don't miss a single interview, article, or magazine photo spread featuring the wit, wisdom, and wackiness of Jim Carrey?

The best way to keep track of Jim's comings and goings is to check out the Jim Carrey fan sites on the World Wide Web. On most of the sites you'll find the latest news about Jim, as well as reprinted magazine articles, sound bites, and even a few trivia games designed to test your Jim Carrey IQ. (The trivia quiz in this book is the perfect practice round for your World Wide Web Jim Carrey challenges!) There are also plenty of chat sites dedicated to conversations about Jim and his career.

Just remember to play it safe when you surf the Net. Never give your address, phone number, or real name to anyone you chat with over the Internet! While you'd like to think that anyone who's a fan of Jim's is a friend of yours, the truth is, some of the people who log on to Internet chat sites are not who they claim to be. People have been known to log on to celebrity and teen-oriented sites just to lure in unsuspecting Internet users. That's why it's so important never to agree to meet or call anyone you've been introduced to over the Internet. In fact, the less personal information you give your fellow chat room visitors, the better.

When searching the Web, you can always find info about Jim's films on their official Web sites. But if you're searching for all Jim all the time, here are some hot sites dedicated to the one, the only Jim Carrey.

FYI: Keep in mind that Web sites come and go. By the time you call it up, one or two of these sites may have disappeared from sight. But more Jim Carrey sites will surely pop up to take their place. Just keep checking the links section of your favorite sites to find out what they are.

All righty, then. Here are the sites to search.

Jim Carrey Heaven
www.welcome.to/jimcarrey heaven

Jim Carrey the King
www.angelfire.com/ny2/JCtheking/index.html

Jim Carrey en Español
clubs.yahoo.com/clubs/jimcarreyenespagol

Wesley's Jim Carrey Page
members.aol.com/funnywes/JimCarrey/JimCarrey.html

Jimmy the Genius
www.geocities.com/Hollywood/Theater/3513/

Maria's Jim Carrey Page
www.angelfire.com/nj3/jameseugenecarrey/

Moviething.com: Jim Carrey, A Biography
moviething.com/bios/jimcarrey

Simone's Jim Carrey Corner
jimcarreyonline.com/simone/Jim/Jim/htm

The Unofficial Jim Carrey Fan Club
w3goodnews.net/~jhenn

Carrey.com: The Jim Carrey Fansite
www.carrey.com

George's Gigantic Jim Carrey Page
geocities.com/Hollywood/Studio/4615/index.html

Jim Carrey Rocks
www.angelfire.com/ms2/jimcarreyrocks

Jim Carrey.HTML
www.geocities.com/Hollywood.Bungalo/4908/jimcar
rey.html

The JIM CARREY Fan page
members.tripod.com/~JimCarrey/index.html

The Zone:Jim Carrey
www.thezone.pair.com/celeb/Carrey.html

The Jim Carrey Experience
www.geocities.com/Hollywood.7993

Jim Carrey Gallery
www.geocities.com/HotSpring/1398/Carrey.html

Jim Carrey World
jimcarreyworld.tripod.com

Jim Carrey's Spotlight
www.geocities.com/SouthBeach/Lights/8037/carrey.
html

The Jim Carrey Area
www.geocities.com/Hollywood/9090/

Jam! Movie Artists:Jim Carrey
jamzhowbiz.com/JamMoviesArtistsC/carrey.html

Absurd Jim Carrey Site
www.resoftlinks.com/cinema/Jim_carrey.shtml

Jim Carrey:The Legend
www.geocities.com/Hollywood/Studio/7678/Jim.html

The Jim Carrey Museum
www.ozis/gunnar/Jim.html

You can reach Jim even if you're not connected to the Net. If you'd like to send him some snail mail, address your envelope to:

Jim Carrey
c/o Nick Stevens
United Talent Agency
9650 Wilshire Blvd.
Suite 500
Beverly Hills, CA 90212

About the Author

NANCY E. KRULIK is the author of more than one hundred books for children and young adults, including the *New York Times* bestsellers *Taylor Hanson: Totally Taylor!* and *Leonardo DiCaprio: A Biography*. She has also written biographies of TV stars Frankie Muniz and Joshua Jackson, and hot pop singers Ricky Martin and JC Chasez. Nancy lives in Manhattan with her husband, composer Daniel Burwasser, and their two children.

Don't Miss a Single Play!

Archway Paperbacks Brings You the Greatest Games, Teams, and Players in Sports!

By

Bill Gutman

☆Football Super Teams

☆Bo Jackson: A Biography

☆Michael Jordan: A Biography (revised)

☆Baseball Super Teams

☆Great Quarterbacks of the NFL

☆Tiger Woods: A Biography

☆ Ken Griffey, Jr.: A Biography

☆ Brett Favre: A Biography

☆Sammy Sosa: A Biography

☆Shaquille O'Neal: A Biography (revised)

An Archway Paperback
Published by Pocket Books

630-13

TV YOU CAN READ

Your favorite shows on WB are now your favorite books.

Look for books from Pocket Pulse™ based on these hit series:

ANGEL™

Buffy the vampire slayer™

Charmed™

Dawson's Creek™

ROSWELL™